TEACHER'S BOOK 1

**Peter Viney
Karen Viney
David P. Rein**

Oxford University Press

Scope and Sequence

	Structures	Functions	Vocabulary	Skills
Introduction *page 1*			•General	
UNIT 1 Fasten your seat belts. *page 4*	•Present simple *to be* •Personal pronouns	•Greetings •Offers	•Countries	•Listening for specific information
UNIT 2 Fast food *page 7*	•Indefinite articles	•Ordering food	•Food •Menus •Numbers •Prices	•Listening for specific information
UNIT 3 Is it a star? *page 10*	•Singular and plural of *to be* with things •*Is it…?/ Are they…?*	•Asking about and identifying objects	•Numbers •Household objects	•Pronunciation of *-s* endings [s], [z], [ɪz] •Spelling rules
UNIT 4 Names and addresses *page 13*	•Possessive adjectives (singular)	•Asking for and giving personal information	•Numbers •Personal information •Sports •Abbreviations	•Reading for specific information •Listening for specific information
UNIT 5 Lambert and Stacey *page 16*	•Possesive adjectives (plural) •Questions •Negatives	•Telling time •Asking and answering questions	•Time	•Reading for specific information
UNIT 6 The train to Chicago *page 19*	•Demonstratives: *this, that, these, those* •*How much…?*	•Asking for directions •Travel arrangements	•Travel	•Listening for specific information •Reading for specific information
UNIT 7 Space station *page 22*	•Indefinite articles: *a/an* vs. definite article *the* •*Wh-* questions •*How old…?*	•Describing people •Asking and answering questions about age	•Nationalities •Professions/jobs •Numbers (four figure)	•Reading for pleasure
UNIT 8 What's it like? *page 25*	•Adjectives	•Describing objects	•Ordinal numbers •Nationalities •Colors	•Reading for specific information

Scope and Sequence

	Structures	Functions	Vocabulary	Skills
UNIT 9 Where is she? *page 28*	•Prepositions of place •*Wh-* questions •Personal pronouns •Object pronouns	•Describing location	•Nationalities	•Listening for specific information
UNIT 10 Quiz of the Week *page 31*	•*There is…/There are…*	•Discussing location	•Household objects	•Writing a list
Checkback Units 1–10 (Review) *page 34*				
UNIT 11 Is there any…? *page 38*	•Countable and uncountable nouns •*Some/any*	•Asking and answering about location of things	•Food •Utensils	•Listening for specific information •Reading from notes •Writing lists
UNIT 12 The Family *page 41*	•Present simple *to have* •Review: Possessive adjectives plus genitive (-'s)	•Discussing relationships •Review: Asking and answering questions about age	•Family	•Reading simple texts
UNIT 13 People *page 44*	•Review: Questions •Present continuous with *wear*	•Describing people	•Color •Clothing •Physical characteristics	•Listening for specific information
UNIT 14 How much is it? *page 47*	•Review: Demonstratives: *this, that, these, those* •Review: Object pronouns	•Asking and answering questions about prices	•Review: Numbers and prices •Food •Size and weight •School/office supplies	•Reading charts
UNIT 15 The keys *page 50*	•Imperatives	•Giving and following instructions	•Household objects	•Writing inventories
UNIT 16 Directions *page 53*	•Imperatives (continued)	•Asking for and giving directions	•Directions •Neighborhood locations	•Reading maps

Scope and Sequence

	Structures	Functions	Vocabulary	Skills
UNIT 17 The Marsh House *page 56*	•Quantity: *How many?*	•Asking about and describing houses/apartments •Review: Greetings	•Housing	•Reading guidebooks •Reading floor plans
UNIT 18 It's mine! *page 59*	•*Whose…?* •*Which one(s)?* •Possessive pronouns	•Discussing ownership	•Supermarket	•Alphabetizing •Scanning for information
UNIT 19 Asking for things *page 62*	•*Would like* •Review: *Wh-* questions	•Requests and offers	•Size and weight •Post office	•Reading reference materials •Reading charts
UNIT 20 Fries with everything *page 65*	•*Could* and *would*	•Review: Ordering food •Requests (continued)	•Menu •Restaurants	•Reading a menu •Listening for specific information
Checkback Units 11–20 (Review) *page 68*				
Story for Pleasure: Air Traffic Control *page 72*	This material can be used as: • Extensive reading for pleasure • Extensive listening for pleasure • Reading comprehension material for review			
Story for Pleasure: Security *page 74*	This material can be used as: • Extensive reading for pleasure • Extensive listening for pleasure • Reading comprehension material for review			

Irregular Verbs *page 76*	**Listening Appendix** *page 77*	**Vocabulary Index** *page 80*	**Grammar Summaries** *page 83*	**Workbook Answer Key** *page 91*

To the Teacher

COURSE COMPONENTS

The components of *Main Street 1* are:

Student Book, with an introductory unit, 20 three-page units, two *Stories for Pleasure*, two *Checkbacks* (review units), an *Irregular Verbs* list, a *Listening Appendix*, a *Vocabulary Index*, and a *Grammar Summaries* section.

Workbook with 20 corresponding units.

Teacher's Book, interleaved with the pages from the Student Book. It contains detailed lesson plans, including notes on the Workbook. The *Listening Appendix, Irregular Verbs* list, *Vocabulary Index*, and *Grammar Summaries* section from the Student Book are included as well as a key to the Workbook exercises.

Audio Cassette or CD, containing recordings of the dialogues, texts, and listening excerises.

■ THE BEGINNER LEVEL

Main Street 1 is designed for beginners. It can be used with a very wide age and ability range. There is no continuing story, and the units are all independent of each other. With false beginners, the material can be used selectively. The materials will be suitable for:

Zero beginners—Students who have studied no English before. With these students, we would suggest sticking closely to the syllabus. We would also suggest using some exercises from the Workbook in class. (See detailed teacher's notes for each lesson.)

Beginners—Students who may have studied English at primary level, or older students who studied a little English several years earlier. Again, we would suggest sticking closely to the syllabus.

False beginners—Students who have studied English in a previous course, but who need to review many of the basics all over again. With these students it is possible to select units, and it is less important to stick rigidly to the progression of the syllabus. Since each unit has a new and discrete story or topic, it will be easy to use the materials selectively. The Workbook can be done outside of class.

■ FIRST PRINCIPLES

We believe that the following points are essential for a successful beginner's course:

A cooperative, non-judgmental atmosphere in the classroom

Students must feel free to experiment with language without fear of ridicule or embarrassment.

An emphasis on communicative goals

We remember seeing two students in a fast food restaurant. One sat with his textbook rehearsing what he was going to say. It took him ten minutes to gain the courage to go to the counter, and say *Excuse me, I would like a cup of coffee, please.* The second student went straight to the counter, nodded and smiled, and said *Coffee*. In terms of communication, the second student was much more successful. The dialogues have been designed with communicative effectiveness in mind.

Transparent teaching points

We leave it up to the teacher to decide whether to introduce grammatical or functional descriptions of the language, and when to introduce them. However, each unit has a clear focus, and the teaching point should be transparent. If you wish to avoid describing the language (either structurally or functionally) you will be able to do so. The students should be able to deduce the point of the lesson. If desired, students can be directed to the Grammar Summaries section at the back of the book.

A clear, carefully-ordered syllabus

The syllabus has interwoven structural and functional elements. It has been designed to follow a clear and logical progression. We have tried to balance the immediate communicative needs with the long-term aims of knowledge of the grammatical system.

Vocabulary development strategies

The importance of vocabulary has been greatly underrated in recent years. It seemed to be forgotten during the 1970s and early 1980s while arguments raged about structural and functional syllabus design. It is important to promote the students' abilities to cope with new and unfamiliar vocabulary items, and to refine their ability to make intelligent guesses. To this end we have made a pragmatic division of the vocabulary in *Main Street 1* into two categories (Active, Passive) and noted where "incidental" vocabulary occurs in reading development work. (See also notes in **The reference section** on page vii.) Both the Student Book and, in particular, the Workbook contain reading and vocabulary development material. The Workbook also contains many exercises designed to review vocabulary.

A balanced approach to skills development

There should be a balance between the skills of listening, speaking, reading, and writing. We are convinced that the Student Book material at the beginner level should be biased towards listening and speaking, though reading and writing should be steadily developed. The Workbook concentrates more on reading and writing. Reading and listening development activities have been included throughout the course, which will enable students to develop their skills in reading and listening to "roughly tuned" materials. There are two *Stories for Pleasure*, where you can choose between using the stories for extensive reading, extensive listening, or intensive reading for comprehension.

Variety of classroom activity

Lessons should not follow a predictable formula. There should be individual solo activities, teacher-centered activities, paired activities, group activities, games, and role plays which involve the whole class.

Varied and interesting contexts

A variety of contexts maintain the students' interest level. Different types of context appeal to different people. Humor has a vital role in language learning, and contexts have been designed to amuse and interest students.

Recognition of the broader educational context

Language learning is not an isolated activity, but a part of a student's general development. Contexts and activities have been designed with this in mind.

Drills and repetition

There is still a place for a mechanical element in a beginner's course. The teaching notes suggest some mechanical activities, such as drills and repetition work. We believe that these help to instill confidence in the students. It should be noted that *everything* we suggest in the teacher's notes is optional. Although we believe that there is a role for mechanical activities (see notes on **Repetition** and **Drills** below), the course can be used successfully without them. Criticism of mechanical activities has led to courses without drills and repetition. As long as these activities are done at a lively pace, are not labored, are not continued to the point of boredom, and are seen as what they are—they are not communication, but a step on the road to eventual communication—they have a purpose in the language teacher's repertoire for the twenty-first century. In several units, drills and repetition work are included for beginners, but there is a note advising teachers of false beginners to skip some of them.

The teacher

We have left the most important element of the course until last. During lesson observation, we have seen the same material taught in a huge variety of styles. There is no *Main Street* style of teaching, in spite of the very detailed plans we have given. One teacher may be extroverted and amusing, another may be quiet and sympathetic, a third may be highly organized and disciplined. You have to make the best of your own personality and beliefs. Books can give plans, but they can never show you how to relate to a number of individuals in a particular place on a particular day. Points to bear in mind are:

1. The ability to listen sympathetically and with interest to your students may be the most important skill of all.

2. Clarity of classroom instruction is essential with beginners. We have done our best to make the printed instructions clear and consistent. It is just as important to be clear and consistent with oral instructions and explanations.

3. Don't set unrealistic goals. Main Street has a spiral progression. Everything will be covered again, and so it is unrealistic to expect perfect accuracy from students, in structure and pronunciation, the first time around. To do so undermines the students' confidence and makes them too self-conscious to aim for communicative goals. Don't set unrealistic goals for yourself either. Don't try to do too much in a lesson. If something comes up which interests all the students, go with it. Leave space to allow yourself to be sidetracked.

4. Accuracy and fluency. There are times in the lesson for both. You can ask for reasonable

accuracy in drills and controlled-question work. However, in role plays, discussions, and free-practice phases of the lesson the aim is not accuracy. It is communication.

5. Feedback. There is a place in the classroom for both confirmation and correction. Students need confirmation when they are performing effectively. Confirmation can be a nod, a smile, or a gesture. You don't have to say *Yes, that's right*. If you use confirmation when things are going well, you may find that the most effective correction device is simply a lack of confirmation. When we are speaking in a foreign language, we often realize we are making mistakes as we make them. Students should have the chance to *self-correct* before you intervene.

6. An open door. We have never observed other teachers without learning something of value. One of the most appealing things about being a teacher is that when you are in class, you are in a private world with your students. The presence of an outsider in this situation is often inhibiting: You don't feel free to make jokes; you find yourself teaching for the observer, not for the class. However, we can all benefit by watching our colleagues, and by having our colleagues watch us. It is worth trying to watch other teachers, and it is worth inviting other teachers to watch you. You may never learn to enjoy the experience, but we are sure that you will find it valuable.

■ THE TEACHER'S BOOK

Lesson plans

The detailed lesson plans for each unit begin with a reference section. We recommend that you read this section before going on to step-by-step notes for each phase of the lesson.

Timing

Each three-page unit has been planned to take an average of 1-1/2 hours in the classroom. In some situations this is the length of a language lesson, in other situations it is a double lesson (two 45-minute periods).

However, the suggested timings will vary widely in different teaching situations. With good false beginners it would be reasonable to expect to cover a unit in one 45–50 minute lesson, and in an intensive course there would be advantages in doing so.

With zero beginners and pre-beginners, it may take longer than 1-1/2 hours to complete a lesson, especially if the Workbook is being used in class. You will need to weigh the desire to exploit the materials thoroughly with the need to cover a given syllabus within the duration of this course. *Main Street* has cyclical review elements throughout. (See the notes on "unrealistic goals" on page vi.) This means that students will have every chance to cover the teaching points again, so you should not labor for perfection on any given point.

The reference section

The reference section at the beginning of each lesson plan is divided into:

Teaching points—These summarize the structural and functional targets of the unit. (See the *Grammar Summaries* section for more details.)

Grammar note—This appears in many units, and comments on the structures being covered.

Expressions—This section lists the formulas and fixed expressions used in the unit. This section is important. We have often used items in this section as formulas before teaching the structure later in the series. For example, students learn *I don't know* early in the series. It is extremely useful, and they are also familiarizing themselves with the form of "simple present negatives" long before they meet the simple present as a structure.

Active vocabulary—This section includes structural terms, and is indexed at the back of the book in the *Vocabulary Index*. However, just because a word is included in this section does not mean that students are expected to "learn" it. We would expect students to become familiar with words by using them. Individual students may wish to memorize words, but this should not be necessary.

Passive vocabulary—This list contains words occurring in texts and dialogues which are necessary for the context of a particular unit, but which students will not be expected to use or recall once the lesson is completed. It is simply enough that students understand these words in context. Some words will appear as "passive" vocabulary in an earlier unit, but will become "active" vocabulary in a later unit. There is no suggestion that words in this section are less useful, less frequent, or less important than those in the active vocabulary section. Their place under passive vocabulary only relates to their use in that particular unit. They are indicated by the letter *P* in the *Vocabulary Index*.

Incidental vocabulary—Some sections are designed to develop reading skills, and therefore contain additional incidental words. These will not be taught, explained, or used in the lesson. They are words that we want students to "read around." They are not listed in the *Vocabulary Index*. Extra vocabulary which may appear in the Workbook, particularly in vocabulary-guessing exercises and reading development material, is also not listed.

Audiovisual Aids—This section notes the audio cassette/CD related to the unit, and lists suggestions for additional visual aids where appropriate. These suggestions are optional.

The step-by-step teaching notes

The sections—The step-by-step notes are divided into clear sections. This makes it easier to plan breaks between the various parts of a unit, and makes the material easier to handle when it is shared between two teachers.

In the lesson plans we have used the following abbreviations: *T* represents the teacher; *C* represents the class in chorus; *S* represents an individual student; and *S1, S2, S3* represent three different individual students.

We hope that the plans are clear and self-evident. The notes below discuss techniques which are used in them. At this point in an introduction many readers are speed reading, or using the introduction to look up a particular point. *Please* read the notes below. They do not (and could not) cover everything which you might do in the classroom, but they do cover some techniques. We are *not* telling you how to teach the course; we are *not* saying that the suggestions below are the best way of teaching a lesson. We would claim that the procedure we suggest gives a thorough and competent route through the materials—but not the only one.

Techniques

Presenting recorded materials

Whenever possible, recorded texts and dialogues should be used in class. The cassette/CD component has a variety of speakers and registers. It has been timed carefully to be towards the lower end of the normal native-speaker speed range. It is not artificially slowed or over-enunciated. Students need to hear a variety of voices. If they are exposed to a natural pace from the beginning, they will accept English at its natural speed from then on.

You can present dialogues yourself (and it may be amusing for your students), but teacher presentation removes both challenge and variety. There may be occasions when equipment is not working or power supplies fail, and then you will have to resort to acting out dialogues yourself. You will also find several small dialogues throughout the text. Some of these are not recorded on the cassette/CD, and you may feel that it would be beneficial to model the conversation for the class before they are expected to say the words themselves.

When playing a recording to a class, be careful not to distract students from the listening task. Don't use the time to write on the board, order your notes, or clean your desk. Move out of eye contact with the class, and listen with them. We do *not* recommend using cassette players with variable-speed controls at any time during the course.

Repetition

Choral repetition gives students a chance to get their tongues around the sound of English words without fear of embarrassment. In a large class, it gives everyone the chance to practice sounds before having to produce them individually.

Ask students to repeat chorally, then follow up the choral repetition by checking a few individuals. Pay attention to stress, rhythm, intonation, and catenation as well as pronunciation.

Wherever possible, have students repeat after the recorded model initially. If their responses are acceptable, move on with the lesson. If there are problems, have them repeat after you, breaking up the sentence by backward build up (backchaining) or foward build up (frontchaining).

For example:

Backward build up
Target sentence: *Would you like a cup of tea?*
Stages: *Would you like a cup of tea?/tea?/cup of tea?/like a cup of tea?/Would you like a cup of tea?*

Foward build up
Target sentence: *I'd like an apple juice.*
Stages: *I'd like an apple juice./I/I'd like/I'd like an apple juice.*

In some units, selective repetition is suggested. This means repeating only the sentences which are part of the teaching points of the lesson, or which have particularly interesting stress and intonation patterns.

The recording tries to demonstrate a range of pronunciation among native speakers.

Some people believe it is important to learn the basic sounds of English perfectly at the beginning of a course. They often get excellent results. However, we feel that over-attention to exact reproduction at the earliest stages leads to embarrassment. Some students genuinely have a "poor ear" for foreign sounds, and they will need time to improve at their own pace. Remember that there is no such thing as English without an accent. We see nothing wrong in people guessing your nationality when you are speaking English, as long as you are clear and comprehensible.

Stress, rhythm, and intonation

During repetition work, stress, rhythm, and intonation are as important as pronunciation. The recording is designed to demonstrate these features of the language. We have avoided the use of stress and intonation diagrams, as they can often cause confusion for students and teachers alike, though occasionally simple arrows can be employed to denote rising or falling intonation. A recording is the best way of noting stress, rhythm, and intonation. If you are happy with diagrams and gestures to demonstrate patterns, use them. If not, concentrate on the recording.

Drills

Drills are not communication, and we would not claim that they are. Drills do, however, give students confidence when the time comes to perform freely, and they maximize student speaking-time in a large class. With very small groups (fewer than seven or eight students) they may be less necessary, although we would still use them. We have deliberately chosen drills which are simple. They are always contextualized. They help to train students to make automatic connections, e.g., between *he* and *she* and *does* and *has*.

Drills operate at a mechanical level, and the mere ability to do a drill is not the aim of any unit in *Main Street*. Drills come early in lessons, and they should be short, contextualized, and done at a lively pace.

The drills should usually be done chorally at first, then individual students should be checked.

There are only six or eight prompts per drill. Even with very large classes, you do not need to extend beyond six or eight prompts in the individual stage. If you do, the drills will become boring.

We suggest the following procedure for doing a drill:

1. Have students repeat the key sentence chorally (*I'd like a cup of coffee.*).

2. Demonstrate how the drill works with examples (two for simple substitution and response drills, three for more complex two/three slot substitutions). Do this by turning your head or body to show that there are two parts to the drill.

   For example, say:
   Teacher: *I*
   Class: *I'd like a cup of coffee.*
   Teacher: *He*
   Class: *He'd like a cup of coffee.*

3. Do the drill chorally at normal speed, remembering that intonation and stress are as important as structure.

   For example:
   Teacher: *I*
   Class: *I'd like a cup of coffee.*
   Teacher: *He*
   Class: *He'd like a cup of coffee.*
   Teacher: *She*
   Class: *She'd like a cup of coffee.*
   etc.

4. Do the drill again, asking six or eight selected individuals. This is the most difficult part of the drill, and drills often become tedious and unchallenging because of the way this stage is handled. The key elements are:

   a. Students must be chosen at random, *never* choose students according to seat order.

   b. The most important part of the individual phase is thinking time. Give the prompt, then pause long enough for everyone in the class to formulate the response mentally, then—and only then—choose an individual at random to respond. In this way, though only six students may actually speak, everyone in the room has been through the process of working out the response.

   c. Even if you only give six prompts to a class of 40, you should occasionally ask the same student to respond twice in a drill. Then students realize that they cannot "switch off" once they have spoken.

Example:

T: *I* (pause, select S1)
S1: *I'd like a cup of coffee.*
T: *He* (pause, select S2)
S2: *He'd like a cup of coffee.*
T: *She* (pause, select S3)
S3: *She'd like a cup of coffee.*
T: *We* (pause, select S1 again)
S1: *We'd like a cup of coffee.*
T: *They* (pause, select S4)
S4: *They'd like a cup of coffee.*
T: *You* (pause, select S5)
S5: *You'd like a cup of coffee.*

Reading aloud

For a teacher, reading aloud is a very important skill. At the beginner level, however, *never* ask students to read aloud in front of the class. Reading aloud presents a bad model; it's boring for the rest of the class; it's something native speakers do badly; and it's unnecessary for students to be able to do unless they are studying for an exam which requires reading aloud. When students do paired reading of a dialogue, they will get sufficient practice in reading aloud without personal embarrassment, without boring other students, and without presenting a bad model.

Reading silently

In most life situations, the natural way to read is silently. Accordingly, students are asked to read texts and dialogues silently, usually after hearing them on tape/CD and having repeated them either from the recording or after the teacher. Sometimes, particularly when a text is designed to enhance reading comprehension, or is explanatory, they are asked to read texts silently before any other work is done.

If students are allowed to ask you questions during a silent reading phase it breaks everyone else's concentration. Encourage them to write down problem words and to read on to the end of the text. Then, when everyone has finished reading, you can answer questions.

Paired reading

Students are asked to read dialogues aloud in pairs. This maximizes student speaking-time, and gives them a chance to move from the printed word to vocalization without the pressure of an audience.

In a two-part dialogue, this will require students to go through the dialogue twice, reversing roles after the first reading. Sometimes paired reading requires students to make controlled substitutions from a list or exercise. When they are making free substitutions, this is a kind of role play (see below). With short, communicatively useful dialogues, you may want to re-enact the dialogue in front of the class with a selected student (for example, a student who has already done it successfully in paired reading). If you do this, it is sometimes a good idea to "stretch" the student's ability by giving unexpected responses: putting him/her into a role-playing situation. For example, the original dialogue may contain this sequence (from Unit 6):

A: *Excuse me, is this the train to Chicago?*
B: *No, it isn't. That's the Chicago train over there.*
A: *Where?*
B: *On track 12.*
A: *Thank you.*
B: *You're welcome.*

If you re-enacted it with a student, it might become:

S: *Excuse me, is this the train to Chicago?*
T: *What? Are you talking to me?*
S: *Yes. Is this the train to Chicago?*
T: *I don't know.*
S: *Uh…you don't know?*
T: *No, I don't. And even if I did, I might not tell you.*
S: *Oh? Why not?*
T: *I'm having a bad day today and I don't feel like talking to anyone!*
S: *Thank you anyway.*

This is an elaborate example, but the same kind of thing can be done in small ways whenever you are practicing a dialogue with a student. The unexpected forces them into using language outside of a controlled situation.

Questions

Questions have two main purposes in the language classroom.

Comprehension questions are based on a text or dialogue, and are a form of controlled language practice. When asking comprehension questions, remember to give everyone in the class time to formulate the answer mentally before selecting an individual student to respond. (See the notes on "thinking time" under **Drills** on page ix.)

Transfer questions are related to the students, and their own experiences, knowledge, or opinions.

In both question types, you should not insist on a fixed answer. If you do so, it becomes a "question drill." Answers like: *I don't know./Maybe./Yes./No./New York./Yesterday* are all genuine answers, which native speakers might use in a given situation.

You can, of course, frame the question so that a particular type of answer becomes *more likely*. (Full question sequences are given in the step-by-step notes.)

Types of questions include:

1. **Yes/No questions.** These questions elicit short responses, and are useful for reviewing the content of text and dialogues, and also for setting up "interactive questions" (see below). Yes/No questions are questions like: *Are you listening?/Do you have a pen?/Do you like tea?/Is he going to call her?/Did she buy any meat?*, etc. The answers tend to be like this: *Yes, I am./No, I'm not./Yes, I do./No, she doesn't./Yes, we did./No, they didn't.*

   The student's task is easier than the content of the questions, while the questions review the information given in a text or dialogue.

2. **Either/or questions.** These questions are artificial, in that they are designed and intended to elicit a full response, and such questions (and full responses) are fairly rare in normal discourse. Examples are: *Does she have a red pen or does she have a blue pen?/Did he go to the bank or did he go to the post office?/Are they in the kitchen or are they in the living room?* The intended answer would be a complete sentence: *She has a blue pen./He went to the bank./They're in the living room.* The students are producing complete sentences, which reproduce the original text.

3. **Wh- questions.** Wh- questions (or "open questions") are questions like: *Where are they?/Who went to the bank?/What are they doing?/How many people are there?/Why is she going to drive to California?* Again, these tend to produce a full answer, though it might often be a short answer. It might elicit: *They're in the living room*, or it might only elicit *The living room*.

4. **Interactive questions.** These are prompts designed to get students to make questions themselves. At the most simple level, you can say *Ask me/him/her/each other*. For example:

   T: *Do you like dancing?*
   S1: *No, I don't.*
   T: (points to S2) *Ask her.*
   S1: *Do you like dancing?*
   S2: *Yes, I do.*
   T: *Juan, do you like dancing?*
   S3: *Sometimes.*
   T: (indicates S4) *Ask me.*
   S4: *Do you like dancing?*
   T: *No, I don't. I've got two left feet! Ask each other.*

   All students ask someone near them, generating informal pair work.

Informal pair work is useful. Don't worry about careful pairing. The prompt *Ask each other* is only used for one or two questions, where it would not be worth setting up formal pairs.

You could vary the questions by adding prompts. For example:

T: *Do you like football?*
S1: *Yes, I do.*
T: *Ask him…"tennis."*
S1: *Do you like tennis?*
S2: *No, not much.*
T: *Ask her "volleyball."*
S3: *Do you like volleyball?*
S4: *No, I don't. I hate volleyball! It's a stupid game.*

We often use slightly more complex interactive questions, such as: *Ask "Where?"/Ask "Who?"/Ask "Why?"/Ask "When?"/Ask "How much?"/Ask "What?"/Ask "Whose?"* etc. These can be set up by deliberately provoking a negative response to a Yes/No question. For example:

T: *Did she go to the post office?*
S1: *No, she didn't.*
T: *Ask "Where?"* (indicate S2)
S2: *Where did she go?* (you indicate S3 with a nod)
S3: *She went to the bank.*
T: *Ask "When?"* (indicate S4)
S4: *When did she go there?* (you indicate S5)
S5: *Yesterday afternoon.*
T: *Ask "Why?"* (indicate S6)
S6: *Why did she go to the bank?* (indicate S2)
S2: *She needed some money.*

Note how much the students said, and how little you said.

Recall activities

Recall activities include "correct these sentences" and "free reproduction."

Correct these sentences can usually be done chorally with the class. You can check one or two individuals. It should not be necessary to allow thinking time as in a drill. For example (from Unit 2):

T: *He wants a hamburger.*
C: *No, he doesn't. He wants a cheeseسandwich.* or *He wants a cheese sandwich.*
T: *Excuse me?* (indicate S1)
S1: *He wants a cheese sandwich.*

Free reproduction is introduced simply by asking: *What's happening?/What's going to happen?/What happened?* Students retell the story.

Listening

Nearly every unit involves listening practice, in that students hear the recording and often do repetition work and drills before they ever see the text. However, by "listening" we mean exercises designed to practice the listening skills.

There are listening exercises at intervals throughout the series which are designated by a cassette symbol. There is a script for these exercises in the *Listening Appendix*. If for some reason you are unable to play the cassette/CD, you can read the listening exercise from the script, although the recording is always preferable.

Listening exercises generally contain a certain amount of incidental material that does not need to be explained or taught in any way. As the listening exercise types vary, procedures are always given in the lesson plans.

If "listening comprehension" is involved, it is best to play the recording through before beginning the exercise. If "listening for specific information" is involved, students may be able to do the exercise "cold." You should explain to students that completion of the set task is *all* that is required of them.

Types of listening exercises include:

Listening for specific information—We concentrate on this skill in the early units so that students become accustomed to approaching a complicated text or dialogue with simple goals in mind. For example, in Units 2, 4, 6, and 20.

One-task listening—Students listen to a fairly long text, with only one task in mind, e.g., working out the winners of a race in Unit 9, or working out who the speakers are talking about in Unit 13.

Following instructions—For example, tracing a route on a map in Unit 16.

Extensive listening for pleasure—This is an optional use of the two *Stories for Pleasure*. You can choose whether to use these stories for reading development or listening development.

Reading development materials

These are always approached through silent reading. There are reading development exercises in many units of the Student Book, together with the two *Stories for Pleasure*. They also occur in the Workbook, increasing gradually in frequency. Exercises include: reading for specific information, reading for gist, unscrambling, matching, multiple choice, cloze exercises, information gap exercises, and a series of game activities such as word search squares, crossword puzzles, and word snakes.

Pair work

In large and small classes, pair work is the only practical way of getting students to use English in a less controlled situation. For very short exchanges you will not need to set up pairs, you can simply say *Ask each other*. (See **Interactive questions** on page xi.)

For longer paired activities it is essential that students should be absolutely clear about the task expected of them in pairs. There are sometimes instructions on the student's page, and you should check that these have been clearly understood.

It is beneficial for students to work with different partners, and pair work can be organized in these ways:

1. Geographically. Students work with neighbors.

2. Streamed. Students work with partners at a similar level.

3. Strong with weak. Stronger students are deliberately paired with weaker ones. Every teacher knows that you often come to understand something fully by explaining it to someone else.

4. Friends. Students choose their own partners.

5. Male/Female. In mixed classes there are advantages in pairing males with females. With younger students, it aids discipline (they are less inclined to chat together) and helps social integration. With older students, it helps with roles in the many male/female dialogues.

There are advantages in all five types of organization. We would suggest using several of them at different times during a lesson.

In some pair work activities students are asked to work alone, drawing up a list for example, before pair work begins. This means that no student is aware of the contents of his or her partner's list, thus creating an *information gap*. The questions asked are then genuine questions—you don't know the answer when you ask the question and you acquire information through your questions.

In other paired activities, students are asked to change partners, so that they can ask about the answers of their partner's previous partner. In simple terms, this encourages third-person questions and answers.

For the same reason, you will often ask students about their partner's answers after a pair-work phase. We have done pair work ourselves with groups of 200. We have seen it done with huge conference audiences—in one case with 2,000 people. It worked.

Group work

The main disadvantage of group work at beginner level is the time that it takes to set up. It is not worth spending 15 minutes to set up a two-minute activity. The first time that you do group work, setting-up time will seem extremely long and perhaps unproductive. But if you are going to use group work frequently throughout a course, the time taken will later prove to be worthwhile.

With very large classes, the disadvantages will usually outweigh the advantages, and you may wish to stick to paired activities. Group work can be used for discussions, games, and role play. Group role plays require time for the characters to be worked out before they are started.

Role play

In role plays, students are asked to adopt the role of a character in a dialogue or situation. They are asked to go through a known dialogue with free substitutions, or to improvise completely freely on a given situation. Students may feel constrained in a situation when they are being themselves. Acting out the role of another person can remove this feeling. There are times when students have to be free to experiment with their abilities in a simulated situation, and role play is an enjoyable and stimulating way of doing it.

What about correction? Role play is a *fluency* activity, not an *accuracy* activity. You should only intervene where the student has failed to communicate. It is best not to make a note of mistakes during the activity. You may wish to comment if a student has repeatedly made the same error, but the comment should come after the activity has finished. If the mistake is important, you will remember it without notes.

Games

Several games are suggested in *Main Street*. Some can be played with the whole class, some can be played in groups. It is up to you whether or not to introduce a competitive element. The class can be divided into teams, and scores can be kept. On the other hand, you may want to avoid a competitive element, and most of the games will work without it.

Discussion

Possibilities for discussion are obviously limited at beginner level. Students should be encouraged to discuss subjects arising from the contexts, and it is surprising how well beginners can often do in a controlled discussion.

The greatest danger of discussion phases is that they can either become a lecture by the teacher, or be dominated by one or two students. One way around this is to get students to discuss in groups before moving to general class discussion. Role-play discussion (where students are given set roles to play) can remove student reluctance to express their own opinions, and, in our experience, role-play discussions often develop into genuine discussions. Of course, discussion is a *fluency* activity. (See notes on correction under **Role play** above.)

Transfer/application

This phase usually begins with a few questions by the teacher about the students' own lives and experiences. Students are using English in a meaningful way, and transfer-question phases often become real discussions. We believe that lessons should be phased so that they end with real communication, whether it is role play, discussion, or transfer-question sessions.

Appendices

The Teacher's Book contains the following appendices from the Student Book:

- **Irregular Verbs**—A list of irregular verbs, including those presented in this series.

- **Listening Appendix**—The scripts for all listening development exercises.

- **Vocabulary Index**—This list is coded into two categories: Active vocabulary and Passive vocabulary. (See page vii.)

- **Grammar Summaries**—An overview of the syllabus, as well as reference material. The *Grammar Summaries* section has been designed with the following points in mind:

   Transparency for the student reader—We have avoided extensive use of metalanguage beyond the students' level at the point at which they first refer to the material.

   Use of labels—We see no need for a student *at this early stage* to worry about labels like subject pronoun, possessive adjective, indefinite article, etc. Nor do we see any need to use functional/notional labels beyond the level of work in the classroom.

   It has always seemed strange to us to waste time and memory learning words like *interrogative* when the perfectly good (and useful) English word *question* covers the same thing.

We have included labels and simple language explanation in the *Grammar Summaries* where we felt some students and teachers might find it helpful. The use of such explanatory material is entirely optional and may be best referred to as a review when the whole course is completed.

Brevity and clarity—We have preferred to put as much information in one paradigm as we can, while remaining consistent with our goal of clarity.

Grammar in context—The paradigms show grammatical items in sentences wherever possible, not as isolated discrete items.

Repetition/recycling—Within the paradigms, previously-covered structures reappear in full in new paradigms which might demonstrate a new element.

The teacher in control—Most importantly, as nearly all of the small amount of grammatical terminology in this series appears in the *Grammar Summaries* and not in the Student Book unit itself, you can decide how much to use with your class. If *Main Street* used grammatical terms extensively, it would control your style of teaching. Students can learn, have learned, and do learn English without relying on metalanguage. Some teachers find it useful, some have an open mind, some find it positively harmful. In this series—because of the amount and placing of grammatical terminology—it is entirely up to *you*, the teacher, to decide on its use or non-use.

In summary, we have taken a positive position on the use of grammar. Language teaching experiences swinging pendulums and changing fashions. Twenty years ago, there was far too much grammar in many classrooms. Ten years ago, at the height of interest in functional/notional syllabus design, there was often too little. As we write this, the popular trend seems to be towards overt grammatical explanation. So, you can add more labels to our paradigms if that suits your teaching style. If, as we expect, future trends lead away from overt explanation, there will be nothing in the series to interfere with your chosen approach. What is presented is the real thing, the essential language itself.

■ CHECKBACK ANSWER KEYS

These appear in the Teacher's Book, interleaved with the *Checkback* units. Note that these answer keys may be copied for use with the *Checkback* units. No other part of *Main Street* may be photocopied without the prior written consent of Oxford University Press.

■ USING THE WORKBOOK

Refer to the notes on **The beginner level** on page v. The Workbook can be used in a number of ways:

1. As homework.
2. In class. If it is used in class, the progression of the course will be slowed. This will make *Main Street* more thorough for beginners. Even with false beginners the Workbook can be useful in class. Many of the activities are suitable for paired oral practice. These are noted in the Teacher's Book.
3. A mixture of 1 and 2 above.

Written exercises

Shorter fill-in exercises can be written in the book. Students should write longer exercises on a separate piece of paper. Shorter exercises can also be copied out in situations where writing in the book is not allowed.

Oral work

Exercises suitable for oral work are always indicated in the lesson plans. They can be integrated into earlier parts of the lesson.

Reading development

Reading development activities are best done at home. Stress to students that all they have to do is complete the set task. They don't have to understand every word.

Writing

There is no "free composition" work in *Main Street 1*. We feel it is unfair to expect students to cope with free composition at this level. They often have to write creative *sentences*, but longer creative work is held back for the later books in the series.

Vocabulary development

Many of the exercises are designed to reinforce vocabulary that has been covered in the Student Book. Other exercises are designed to help students guess unfamiliar words. There is a strong recycling element.

Sounds and spelling

The sounds exercises can be done without oral checking, but we would advise oral explanation in class, and oral checking in class. The actual exercise can be done at home. The spelling exercises should be self-explanatory.

Workbook answer key

There is a key to the Workbook exercises at the back of this book.

Reading outside the classroom

We would recommend using graded readers in a library system toward the end of the course. You will probably want to select from a wide range of reading materials. Check to ensure that the level of the reading materials matches that of *Main Street 1*.

We believe that students should have access to a library of supplementary graded readers wherever possible. We also believe that reading outside the classroom increases as checking back by the teacher decreases. Let students choose a reader, and feel free to ignore the exercises provided with it.

Reference material

We recommend the *Oxford ESL Dictionary for Students of American English*. However, since this is an intermediate level dictionary, students might also consider the simpler 2,400 word *New Oxford Picture Dictionary* for *Main Street* Levels 1 and 2. Another alternative for these first two levels is the *Oxford Elementary Learner's Dictionary* (10,000 words). Note, however, that this is a British English dictionary, and that there will be spelling differences. By the third level of *Main Street*, the more comprehensive *Oxford ESL Dictionary* will be more appropriate. *The Oxford Picture Dictionary* (2,000 words) is also useful at the early levels and uses both American and British English.

Final note

We are always interested in feedback from teachers. If you have any suggestions or comments on any of the materials in *Main Street 1*, please write to us.

Peter Viney, Karen Viney, and David P. Rein
c/o ESL Department
Oxford University Press
200 Madison Avenue
New York, NY 10016

Introduction

■ **GENERAL NOTE**

This unit is an *optional* introduction to the series. It may be used in the following ways:

Use this lesson in classes for true beginners.

With false beginners in a specialized language school, use this lesson as homework *after* completing Unit 1 of the course.

With false beginners in a normal school, have students look over the lesson prior to their work in Unit 1. Encourage students to ask questions about the content of the Introduction during your first class meeting.

The following notes are for those who wish to use this material in class.

■ **ORAL INTRODUCTION**

1. Teach *Hello.* Say it to as many students as possible, getting them to respond. Shake hands. Get students to circulate around the class, shaking hands and saying *Hello.*

2. For the rest of this lesson, use as much mime and gesture as possible, getting students to follow your instructions and examples in English. Speak as you demonstrate with gestures: *Open your books.* (Check that students do so.) *Close your books.* (Check that students do so.)
Continue: *Open your books. Close your books. Open your books. Close your books. Open your books. Good. Thank you. Look at this page.* (Hold up your book, indicate, check that students follow the directions.)
Continue: *Look at this page. Good. Thank you.*

3. Point to a word on the page *(taxi)*. Say: *taxi*. Scratch your head, search among the pictures on the page, find the taxi, smile broadly, and draw an imaginary line with your finger between the word and the picture. Say: *taxi!* Indicate that students should do the same. Make a *Shhh!* noise and gesture and demonstrate someone silently matching words and pictures.

A. English words

Have students work alone to match the words to the pictures. Check them with the class. Point out that they already "know" 24 English words.

Main Street

Introduction

A English words

Match words and pictures.

- [ ] taxi
- [ ] jet
- [ ] television
- [ ] bus
- [ ] satellite
- [ ] helicopter
- [ ] cassette
- [ ] telephone
- [ ] film
- [ ] computer
- [ ] video
- [ ] camera
- [ ] disk
- [ ] pizza
- [ ] calculator
- [ ] tennis
- [ ] football
- [ ] theater
- [ ] hot dog
- [ ] hamburger
- [ ] sandwich
- [ ] restaurant
- [ ] police officers
- [ ] supermarket

English	My language		English	My language
telephone	_____		sports	_____
television	_____		pizza	_____
radio	_____		taxi	_____
computer	_____		football	_____
cassette	_____		tennis	_____
camera	_____		police	_____
film	_____		hamburger	_____
sandwich	_____		buffet	_____
restaurant	_____		coffee	_____
disk	_____		jeans	_____

■ PHOTOGRAPHS

This exercise deliberately uses photographs from different countries, to show that most languages have words in common with English. Have students study the photographs and mark the "English" words. Again use demonstration and mime to indicate this.

English/My language

1. This is the only translation exercise in the series. The purpose of the translation is to bring out similarities, not differences. Often the difference will be simply spelling changes.

2. Have students work alone on this exercise.

3. Alternatively, have students work in pairs. Tell students that they can speak in their native language for this particular exercise, but future pair work will be done only in English.

B. English word square

1. Have students examine the word square. Explain how to find words horizontally and vertically. If necessary, give specific examples.

2. Have students work alone on this exercise.

3. Check answers. The answers we anticipate from beginners are:
   1) football 2) jet 3) yes 4) taxi 5) video 6) film
   7) disk 8) sandwich 9) no 10) jeans
   11) computer(s) 12) television 13) radio
   14) police 15) tennis.

   Additional possible answers are:
   16) foot 17) ball 18) tax 19) it 20) ten 21) art
   22) by 23) bye 24) sand 25) pat 26) lice 27) put
   28) ice 29) vision 30) air 31) and 32) so
   33) Levi's® 34) all

C. More English words?

Have students write any more English words that they know. Encourage students to examine the large illustration at the bottom of the page. The picture may give them some ideas.

■ CLOSURE

Teach students the word *Good-bye*. Say it to as many students as possible, getting them to respond.

B English word square

Find English words.

8 = good, **10** = very good, **14** = fantastic!

```
F O O T B A L L G P
H C J E T I Y E S O
J O O L E R M B J L
E M V E P A T A X I
A P W V I D E O B C
N U L I A I N U Y E
S T X S R O N O E K
D E J I T F I L M Z
N R Q O D I S K F C
S S A N D W I C H J
```

C More English words?

Write ten English words.

1. _____
2. _____
3. _____
4. _____
5. _____
6. _____
7. _____
8. _____
9. _____
10. _____

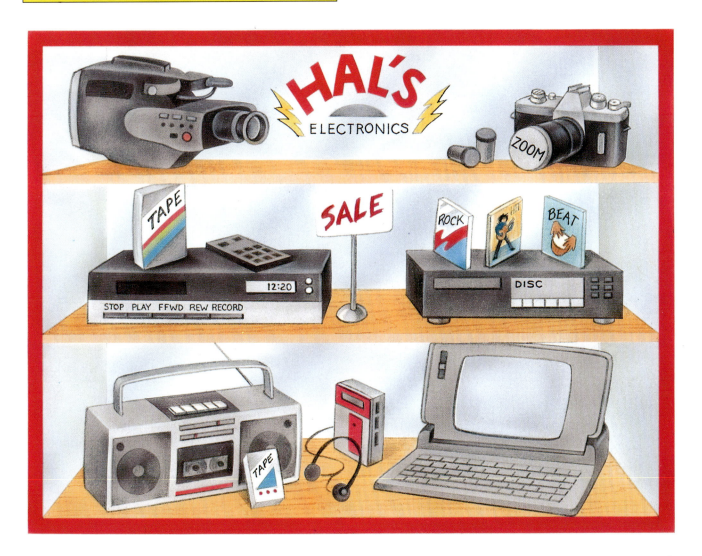

3

1 Fasten your seat belts.

10 ten	5 five
9 nine	4 four
8 eight	3 three
7 seven	2 two
6 six	1 one

A I'm Peter Wilson.

Look at the picture. Listen. Find the speakers. Write 3, 4, 7, 8, 9, and 10.

1 Coffee?
2 Yes, please.
1 A sandwich?
2 No, thank you.

☐ Hello.
☐ Hello.
☐ Are you from the United States?
☐ Yes, I am.

5 Hello.
6 Hello.
5 I'm Peter Wilson.
6 I'm Sarah Kennedy.

☐ Are you from Canada?
☐ No, I'm not.
☐ Oh? Where are you from?
☐ I'm from Australia.

☐ Look! That's Maria Jackson!
☐ Maria Jackson? Is she famous?
☐ Yes, she is.
☐ Where's she from?
☐ She's from Hollywood!

4

1 Fasten your seat belts.

Teaching points
Verb *to be* singular forms, personal names, countries
Names of countries:
England/Canada/Brazil/Australia/Mexico/Japan/the United States/Italy/Greece/France and countries of your students
Numbers 1–10
Greetings and offers
I'm/You're/He's/She's from (the United States).
I'm not/You aren't/He isn't/She isn't from (the United States).
Am I/Are you/Is he/Is she from (the United States)?
Yes, I am./No, I'm not.
Yes, you are./No, you aren't.
Yes, he is./No, he isn't.
Yes, she is./No, she isn't.
Where am I/are you/is he/is she from?
Listening: matching dialogues to pictures

Expressions
Hello.
Coffee? (offer)
Yes, please./No, thank you.
Oh?

Active vocabulary
am ('m)/are ('re)/coffee/famous/from/he/I/is ('s)/look (at)/no/not (n't)/sandwich/she/that/the/where/yes/you

Passive vocabulary
and/classmate/conversation/country (nation)/emergency/exit/fasten/find/listen (to)/match (v.)/name/people/picture/seat belt/speaker/talk (to)/think of/your

Audiovisual aids
Cassette/CD
Expansion: world map, blank cards, flash cards of food items or real items

■ ORAL INTRODUCTION

1. Say: *Hello.* Encourage the class to say *Hello* in chorus. Say *Hello* to individual students to elicit *Hello* in response.

2. Say: *I'm (Susan Brown).* Stand before individual students and say, *I'm (Susan Brown).* Make a gesture to indicate that you want the students to respond: *I'm (Carlos Sanchez),* etc.

3. Distribute blank cards to all students. Instruct them to write their own names on the cards. Demonstrate by writing your own name on a paper or card. Say: *Write.* Put the card on your desk. Circulate around the class to check students' comprehension and accuracy. Tell students to put their name cards on their desks.

4. Say: *He's (Carlos Sanchez). She's (Marie Lebrun).* Continue doing this with four or five names. Say: *Repeat!* Go through all the names again. Encourage students to repeat the sentences in chorus.

5. Move around the class and stop in front of individual students. Say: *You're…?* Prompt the student to reply: *I'm (Yoko Kawasaki).*

6. Indicate individual students and say: *He's….* Pause and indicate to the class that you don't know the student's name. Have the class finish the sentence: *He's (Mario Russo). She's (Yoko Kawasaki).* Indicate yourself and say: *I'm…?* to elicit: *You're (Susan Brown).*

■ NUMBERS 1–10

1. Teach the numbers 1–10. Write the numbers on the board and say them aloud. Point to the numbers in order and say them aloud again. Say: *Repeat!* Indicate that you want the students to repeat after you.

2. Point to numbers in random order and have students repeat the numbers in chorus. Then point to numbers and encourage the class to call out the numbers in chorus. Repeat this procedure with individual students.

3. Have students open their books. Say: *Look at Unit 1.* Then point out the box of numbers at the top of the page. Have students look over the numbers silently.

4. Write out the numbers 1–10 in words on the board (*one, two, three,* etc.). Repeat the same procedure you followed above.

continued

A. I'm Peter Wilson.

1. Say: *Look and listen.* Indicate your eyes as you say *Look* and your ears as you say *Listen.* Play the recording for all the small dialogues on the page.

2. Demonstrate the meaning and purpose of the exercise. Show the students that the characters numbered 1 and 2 are the speakers in the first dialogue. The numbers are written in the boxes as an example. Explain that students are to fill in the boxes for the rest of the dialogues on the page. (Boxes for characters 5 and 6 have also been filled in.)

3. Play the recording again. Have students complete the exercise on their own. If necessary, play it a third time. Have students exchange books to check answers or check the answers yourself.

■ DIALOGUE 1 (1, 2)

Coffee?/Yes, please…

1. Play the recording. Play it again, pausing for students to repeat, chorally and individually. Point out the intonation of questions: *Coffee? A sandwich?* Ask students to raise their hands when they hear your voice change.

2. Paired Reading. Divide the class into pairs. Indicate a pair and say: *You're one, you're two.* Demonstrate how to act out the dialogue. Encourage students not to look at their books so that the dialogue feels more natural. Say: *Now you're two, and you're one.* Have students switch roles and say the dialogue again. Have all pairs in the class read through the dialogue simultaneously in this manner.

3. Pair Work. Have students substitute other items. Write some suggestions on the board: *Tea? Soda? Pizza? Candy?* Concentrate on items that are popular in the students' country.

4. Expansion. Use flash cards with names of food items on them. Pass them around the class and have students ask each other if they want the item. Elicit: *Yes, please./No, thank you.*

■ DIALOGUE 2 (3, 4)

Hello/Hello/Are you from the United States?

1. Play the recording. Play it again, pausing for students to repeat, chorally and individually.

2. Paired Reading. Follow directions above.

3. Pair Work. Have students substitute their own country in the dialogue.

■ DIALOGUE 3 (5, 6)

Hello/Hello/I'm Peter Wilson….

1. Play the recording. Play it again, pausing for students to repeat, chorally and individually.

2. Paired Reading. Follow directions above.

3. Pair Work. Have students substitute their own names and continue to work on the dialogue.

4. Class Work. Have students circulate around the classroom in order to introduce themselves to each other and to you. Encourage them to act out the situation and shake hands as they make introductions.

Culture note: Mention the importance of shaking hands in social and business situations. Demonstrate a "good," hearty handshake. Explain that weak handshakes are a reflection upon the person's personality. People often regard others who shake hands in a lame manner as unfriendly, dispassionate, and unenthusiastic. It is always better to shake hands heartily, and it is also wise to make eye contact as well.

■ DIALOGUE 4 (7, 8)

Are you from Canada?/No, I'm not….

1. Play the recording. Play it again, pausing for students to repeat, chorally and individually.

2. Paired Reading. Follow directions above.

3. Pair Work. Have students substitute their own country in the dialogue.

4. Class Work. Have students circulate around the classroom. Have them practice Dialogues 2 and 3.

■ DIALOGUE 5 (9, 10)

Look! That's Maria Jackson!

1. Play the recording. Play it again, pausing for students to repeat, chorally and individually. Point out the different ways in which Maria Jackson is said.

2. Paired Reading. Follow directions above.

3. Pair Work. Have students substitute the names of students in class.

continued

B Match.

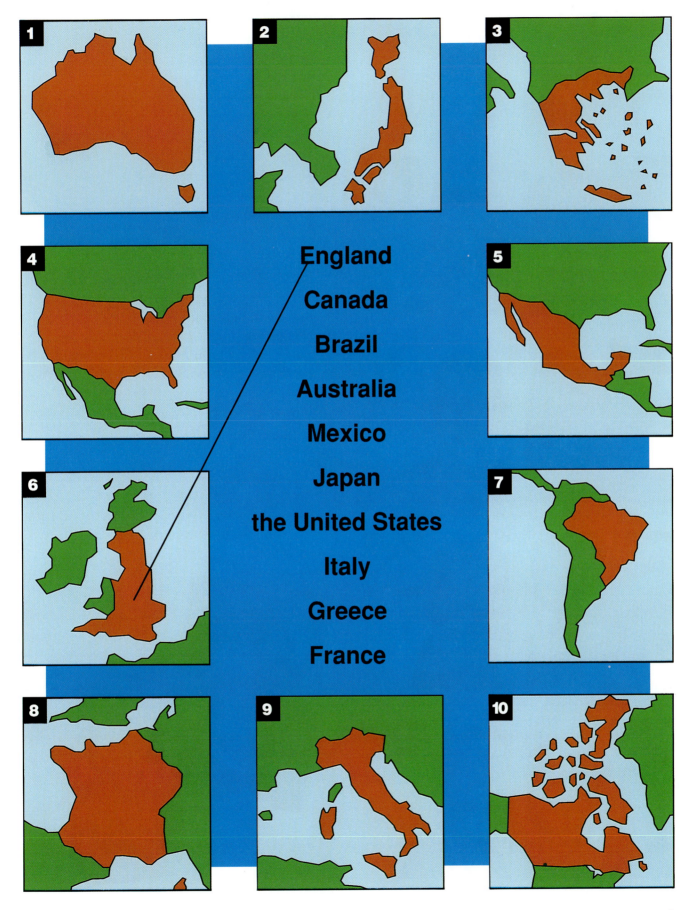

England

Canada

Brazil

Australia

Mexico

Japan

the United States

Italy

Greece

France

5

Peter Wilson

Sarah Kennedy

Monique Lefort

Yuriko Tanaka

Maria Jackson

João Medeiros

Pedro García

Paola Bonetti

Hal Whitefoot

Eleni Dima

C Where's he from?/Where's she from?

1. Look at the pictures. Make conversations.

A: That's Paola Bonetti.
B: Is she from the United States?
A: No, she isn't.
B: Is she from Italy?
A: Yes, she is.

C: That's Hal Whitefoot.
D: Where's he from?
C: He's from Canada.

2. Talk to your classmates.

E: Hello.
F: Hello.
E: I'm (name).
F: I'm (name).

G: Are you from (country)?
H: No, I'm not.
G: Where are you from?
H: I'm from (country).

3. Think of famous people.

I: Is Midori from Japan?
J: Yes, she is.

K: Is Tom Cruise from Canada?
L: No, he isn't.
K: Where's he from?
L: He's from the United States.

B. Match.

1. Point out the ten pictures on the page. Have students draw arrows between the country names and country maps.

2. Have students exchange books to check answers.

3. Circulate around the classroom to check answers yourself.

4. Have students repeat the country names after you.

5. Expansion. Using a world map, point out various countries. Ask for volunteers to point to countries that they know. Write the names of the countries on the board and have students repeat after you.

C. Where's he from?/Where's she from?

1. Point to the picture of Paola Bonetti. Model the conversation between A and B. Demonstrate various substitutions: *Is she from England? Canada? Brazil?*, etc.

2. Pair Work. Have students work on the dialogue and substitutions, switching roles. Ask volunteers to demonstrate the conversation in front of the class.

3. Model the conversation between C and D. Again, have students work on the conversation and substitutions, switching roles.

4. Model the conversation between E and F. Put students into pairs to practice the conversation. Have students move around the classroom and demonstrate the conversation.

5. Model the conversation between G and H. Have students substitute their own country names.

6. Say: *I'm a teacher.* Indicate a student: *She's a student. He's a student.*
   Ask questions to individuals: *Is he a teacher? Is she a student?* to elicit: *Yes, he is./No, he isn't. Yes, she is./No, she isn't.*
   Ask: *Am I from (the United States)?/Am I a student?/Am I a teacher?* to elicit: *Yes, you are./No, you aren't.*
   Have students ask similar questions about themselves to elicit: *Yes, you are./No, you aren't.*
   Ask: *Am I from (Japan)? Am I from (Italy)? Is he from (Mexico)? Is she from (the United States)? Are you from (Brazil)?* to elicit short answers. Do this with several individuals for each question type.

7. Model the conversation between I and J. Have students brainstorm the names of other famous people. Write the names on the board. Encourage students to practice the dialogue with other names.

8. Model the conversation between K and L. Have students follow the same pattern as indicated above.

   Culture note: Midori is a famous musician from Japan and Tom Cruise is a famous movie star from the United States.

9. Drill. See the Introduction regarding drills.

   T: *you*
   C: *Where are you from?*
   Continue with other pronouns or names: *he/she/Peter Wilson/Sarah Kennedy.*

10. Comprehension Dictation. Dictate the numbers 1 to 10 in random order: *5, 9, 1, 4, 10, 2, 8, 6, 3, 7.* Have students write their answers in numeric form (*1, 2, 3*, etc.).

11. Expansion. Make a list of currently famous people and their country of birth. You might need to prepare this before the lesson. Divide the class into small groups and simulate a quiz show. Ask questions about the people on your list. Groups that correctly identify the birthplaces of ten people, win the game.

■ WORKBOOK

The Workbook can be done for homework and checked in class. If you wish to use it in class, Exercises C and D can be done as oral pair work. Only one student needs to have the book open. Students can write their answers, switch roles, and redo the exercises.

2 Fast food

Teaching points
Simple restaurant situations, asking for things, greetings
Numbers 11–20, 30, 40, 50, 60, 70, 80, 90
and
Indefinite article: *a/an*
a hamburger/an ice cream cone
Listening for specific information
Reading selectively from lists
Vocabulary set: foods, menus

Expressions
Good morning./Good night.
OK.
Anything else?
That's ($6).
Here you are./There you go./Here you go.
Thanks.
Thank you.
You're welcome.
Can I help you?
uh... (hesitation)
Have a nice day!
Hi. (informal hello)
Excuse me?
How are you?
Fine, thanks. And you?

Active vocabulary
*a/an/and/apple/cheese/chicken/chocolate/dollar/egg/fine/
fries/fruit/hamburger/ice cream cone/milk/oh/orange/pie/
salad/soda/tuna*
OK.
Numbers: 11–20, 30, 40, 50, 60, 70, 80, 90

Passive vocabulary
*beverage/box/cake/cheeseburger/cherry/check/correct/
dessert/fast/food/in/lettuce/onion ring/shake/side
order/tea/tomato/vanilla*

Audiovisual aids
Cassette/CD
Expansion: Flash cards of food items

■ ORAL INTRODUCTION

1. Say *Good morning* (or *Good afternoon/evening* as appropriate). Encourage the class to respond in chorus. Elicit the correct greeting from individual students.

2. Say the numbers 11–20 out loud. Write the numbers on the board and point to them at random. Get students to respond with the appropriate number.

3. Comprehension Dictation. Say the numbers in correct order and have students write them down. Then say the numbers out of order and have students write them down. Check answers.

A. Food

1. Have students open their books. Talk about the picture. Ask students if they are familiar with any of the pictured items. Write the names of the items on the board.

2. Read the names of the items aloud. Have students repeat after you.

3. Model the example. Point out number 11 in the picture and its counterpart in the list below *(sandwich)*. Explain that they have to match the remaining items in the list with the pictured items.

4. Do an oral matching activity. Say: *Eleven*. Elicit the response: *Sandwich*. Continue with all pictured items.

5. Reverse the process. Say: *Sandwich*. Elicit the response: *Eleven*.

Fast food

11 eleven	16 sixteen
12 twelve	17 seventeen
13 thirteen	18 eighteen
14 fourteen	19 nineteen
15 fifteen	

A Food

Look at 11 in the picture. Write 12, 13, 14, 15, 16, 17, 18, and 19.

11 eleven: a sandwich
12 twelve: a hamburger
13 thirteen: a fruit salad
14 fourteen: an apple
15 fifteen: an orange
16 sixteen: an ice cream cone
17 seventeen: pie
18 eighteen: coffee
19 nineteen: soda

20 twenty   **30** thirty   **40** forty   **50** fifty   **60** sixty   **70** seventy   **80** eighty   **90** ninety

SANDWICHES	**$2.50**	**BEVERAGES**	
CHEESE	CHICKEN SALAD	TEA	.60
TUNA	EGG SALAD	COFFEE	.80
		SODA	.90
SALADS	**$1.80**		
FRUIT		**DESSERTS**	
LETTUCE AND TOMATO		ICE CREAM CONES	$1.10
		PIE	$1.20
FRUIT	**.50**		
APPLE	BANANA		
ORANGE			

11: Good morning.
12: Good morning. A cheese sandwich, please.
11: OK. Anything else?
12: Yes, coffee.
11: Here you are.
12: Thanks.
11: You're welcome.

13: Can I help you?
14: An egg salad sandwich, please, and…uh…a tuna sandwich.
13: There you go. Anything else?
14: Yes, an apple and an orange.
13: That's six dollars…. Thank you. Have a nice day!

■ NUMBERS 20–90

1. Have students look over the numbers silently. In addition, have them review the numbers 11–19 on the previous page.

2. Aural Discrimination. Put two columns on the board. Label the columns A and B. Write 13, 14, 15, 16, 17, 18, 19 under column A. Write 30, 40, 50, 60, 70, 80, 90 under column B.
   Call out all of the numbers in random order and have students respond with the correct column.

   T: *thirteen*   C: *A*
   T: *thirty*   C: *B*
   Continue with the remainder of numbers in both columns.

3. Comprehension Dictation. Call out some of the numbers. Have students write them down in numeric form *(13, 40, 15,* etc.).

■ CONVERSATION 1 (11, 12)

1. Have students look at the picture of the conversation between 11 and 12.

2. Demonstrate how to cover the appropriate conversation (text) while looking at the pictures. Explain that this technique will be used throughout the series. Students need to know that they will only be concentrating on the illustration and not the written text.

3. Play the recording. Play it again, pausing for students to repeat, chorally and individually.

4. Model the phrase: *Here you are* by passing an object to a student while saying it. Indicate that students should pass it around the classroom and that they should always say *Here you are.*

5. Have students uncover the text and read the first conversation silently.

6. Paired Reading. Divide the class into pairs and have them read the conversation together. Then have students reverse roles.

7. Direct students' attention to the menu. Allow students to read it silently.

8. Ask comprehension questions about the contents of the menu: *What kind of sandwiches are on the menu? What kind of beverages are served? Can you get a fruit salad? Can you buy ice cream cones here?*

9. Model the correct phrasing of the prices on the menu. *($2.50 = Two dollars and fifty cents/$1.80 = One dollar and eighty cents/$.50 = Fifty cents,* etc.) Have students repeat chorally and individually. Note the vocabulary words that pertain to coins in the United States: *nickel (5¢)/dime (10¢)/quarter (25¢).*

10. Drill the prices on the menu:

    T: *salads*
    C: *$1.80*
    T: *pie*
    C: *$1.10*

11. Expansion. If possible, use food flash cards of some of the items on the menu. Ask: *What's this?* Check comprehension. Encourage students to draw their own food flash cards or cut out pictures from magazines or newspapers to practice additional comprehension of everyday food items.

12. Pair Work. Have students role play the dialogue and substitute other items from the menu. Encourage them to act out the dialogue rather than read it from the book.

■ CONVERSATION 2 (13, 14)

1. Follow the same procedure as for Conversation 1 (steps 1, 2, 3, 5, 6).

2. Explain indefinite articles: *a/an.* Model some examples of words that are preceded by *an: apple, egg, ice cream cone, orange, umbrella.* Note: You may have to draw some of these items on the board for clarification. Also model words that are preceded by *a: sandwich, hamburger,* etc.

3. Explain that the expression *There you go* means the same as *Here you are.*

4. Drill. Call out a variety of food items from the menu and have students respond by adding the indefinite article:

   T: *apple*
   C: *an apple*

Culture note: Fast food restaurants are very popular in the United States. These restaurants generally serve items that can be eaten in the car, although many people rely on the fast service in order to bring dinner home to their families to avoid meal preparation time.

continued

5. Expansion. Talk about the conversations in the fast food restaurant. Demonstrate the difference between *polite* and *rude*. Ask for a volunteer to role play the conversation with you. Change the inflection in your voice to show a rude restaurant employee: *Can I help you?* (Make a scowling face to get the meaning across.) Interrupt the student. Act very impatient as you are "taking the order." Change the inflection in your voice when you say: *Anything else?* Do not thank the student and do not wish them a nice day. Encourage students to brainstorm additional phrases that might be said in a similar situation. Write them on the board.

■ CONVERSATION 3 (15, 16)

1. Follow the same procedure as for Conversation 1 (steps 1, 2, 3, 5, 6).

2. Model the phrase: *Excuse me?* Explain that this phrase is an excellent way to get someone to repeat something. Point out that the waiter didn't understand what the customer was ordering. By saying *Excuse me*, the waiter is able to hear the order again.

3. Ask volunteers to say something to you. (*My name is Maria Perez.*, *A cheese sandwich, please.*, and so on.) Once the student has spoken, say: *Excuse me?* Look confused. Have students repeat their sentences. Repeat what they have said to you for further clarification.

4. Pair Work. Have students practice asking for clarification.

5. Point out that the expression *Here you go* is another variation of *Here you are* and *There you go*. The three expressions can be used interchangeably.

6. Point out the greetings in the conversation. Demonstrate the difference between greeting someone upon arrival (*Hi. Hello. Good morning. Good afternoon. Good evening*) and departure (*Good-bye. Good night*) by going in and out of the classroom. Say: *Hi!* and so on, when you enter the room. Say: *Good-bye* or *Good night* when you leave the room.

7. Have students practice "arriving" and "departing." Check comprehension by practicing with them.

8. Read the prices on the menu aloud. Check students' comprehension by calling out specific prices and have students tell you the name of the item that costs that amount.

■ CONVERSATION 4 (17, 18)

1. Follow the same procedure as for Conversation 1 (steps 1, 2, 3, 5, 6).

2. Model the phrase: *How are you?* Elicit a response from a student: *Fine, thanks.*

3. Brainstorm a number of responses to the question: *How are you?* Write them on the board. (*Not bad. Pretty good. Excellent! Just great! Fantastic!*)

   Culture note: Point out that people generally respond positively to this question whether or not they are actually feeling/doing fine. Explain that most people are not really interested in hearing about bad news or minor everyday problems.

4. Have students circulate around the class and greet each other. Encourage them to use some of the phrases that you brainstormed above.

■ A/AN

1. Have students read the *a/an* comparison chart. Point out the examples that show when to use *a*, *an*, and no article.

2. Write *a, e, i, o,* and *u* on the board. Explain that most words that begin with these letters use the word *an*.

B. Four conversations

1. Explain the format of this kind of listening task. Tell students that they will be listening to four conversations on the recording. They need to listen carefully and "take the orders" that they will hear.

2. Play the recording once so that students will become acquainted with the various voices. Point out again that students do not need to listen to each and every word. They simply need to listen for the information that they need in order to check off the information on the "order form."

3. Play the first conversation again and shut off the tape/CD player. Show students the example in the book.

4. Play the other three conversations, stopping the tape/CD player after each one. Have students complete the chart with the orders that they heard.

5. Play the conversations once again. Have students check their answers.

■ WORKBOOK

The Workbook can be done for homework and checked in class. If you wish to use it in class, Exercises C and D can be used as oral pair work. Only one student needs to have the book open. Students can write their answers, switch roles, and redo the exercises.

15: Hi. Can I help you?
16: A hamburger, please.
15: Excuse me?
16: A hamburger, please, and fries.
15: A hamburger and fries. Anything else?
16: An ice cream cone, please. Chocolate.
15: That's $4.50…. Here you go.
16: Thank you. Good night.
15: Good night.

a	an	
a hamburger	an apple	coffee
a cheese sandwich	an orange	milk
a salad	an ice cream cone	pie

B Four conversations

Listen to the four conversations. Check (✓) the correct boxes.

17: Hello, John.
18: Hello, Daniel. How are you?
17: Fine, thanks. And you?
18: I'm fine.
17: And Stephen? How's he?
18: Oh, he's fine.

	1	2	3	4
Salads				
fruit	✓			
chicken				
tuna				
lettuce and tomato				
Sandwiches				
cheese				
tuna				
egg salad				
chicken salad				
Beverages				
coffee				
tea				
milk	✓			
shake				
soda				
Desserts				
apple pie				
ice cream				
chocolate cake	✓			

3 Is it a star?

1.

Pete: Look!
Dave: Where?
Pete: Over there. What is it?
Dave: I don't know. Is it an airplane?
Pete: No, it isn't an airplane. Is it a star?
Dave: No, it isn't. What is it, Pete? Is it a UFO?
Pete: I don't know, Dave…I don't know.

2.

Al: Is it open?
Bill: Yeah, it's open.
Al: Are they radios?
Bill: No, they aren't radios.
Al: What are they? Are they CD players?
Bill: No, they aren't. They're VCRs, and computers, and—
Al: Listen! What's that?
Bill: Oh no! It's a police car!

Is it a star?

> **Teaching points**
> Singular and plural nouns
> Verb *to be* (*it* and *they* for things)
> Identifying objects with:
> *What is it?/What are they?*
> *It's/isn't a pen/an engine.*
> *They're/They aren't pens/engines.*
> *Is it a pen/an engine?*
> *Are they pens/engines?*
> *Yes, it is./No, it isn't.*
> *Yes, they are./No, they aren't.*
> *Where?*
> Plurals—formation.
> Pronunciation of *-s* endings [s], [z], [ɪz].
> pen/pens key/keys watch/watches dictionary/dictionaries
> knife/knives man/men woman/women
> Numbers: 20–99
>
> **Grammar note: Indefinite articles** *(a/an)*
> The rule that *an* is used before a/e/i/o/u is important (see Unit 2), but it is necessary for students to understand that it is the sounds a/e/i/o/u rather than the letters. With false beginners, point out *an umbrella* (sound [ə]), but *a university* (sound: [yü]). Likewise, we say *an H* but *a U*. Stating this rule would confuse a beginner's class. See **Plural Spellings/Pronunciation** below.
>
> **Expressions**
> *Over there.*
> *I don't know.*
> *Yeah* (informal *yes*)
> *Oh, no!*
>
> **Active vocabulary**
> airplane/book/bus/car/cassette player/CD player/computer/cup/dictionary/engine/fork/glass/island/it/key/knife/man/open/orchestra/pen/picture/plate/police car/radio/speaker/spoon/star/they/TV/UFO/umbrella/VCR/watch/what/woman
>
> **Passive vocabulary**
> between/Bingo/close/for/game/minute/number/partner/play/student/study/teacher/with
>
> **Audiovisual aids**
> Cassette/CD
> Realia: as many objects pictured on page 11 as possible

■ ORAL INTRODUCTION

1. Use realia to teach: *What is it? It's a (pen). What are they? They're (pens).* Use an assortment of real items (two of each) that are pictured on page 11: forks, spoons, knives, cups, plates, glasses, pens, books, dictionaries, umbrellas. In addition, include items that are not pictured: envelopes, pencils, rulers, batteries, cassettes, and so on.

2. Hold up a single item and ask: *What is it?* Model the answer: *It's (a book).* Encourage students to respond in chorus: *It's (a book). It's (an umbrella).* Continue this practice until students feel comfortable with singular nouns.

3. Hold up two items and ask: *What are they?* Model the response: *They're (books). They're (umbrellas).* Encourage students to respond in chorus: *They're (books). They're (umbrellas).* Continue this practice until students feel comfortable with plural nouns.

■ CONVERSATION 1 (Pete/Dave)

1. Have students look at the picture.

2. Review the technique of covering the conversation (text) while looking at the picture. Emphasize that you only want the students to think about the picture at this time. They are not required to read the conversation(s).

3. Play the recording. Play it again, pausing for students to repeat after each line, chorally and individually.

4. Demonstrate the meaning of the phrase: *Over there.* Point to the distance and say: *Over there!*

5. Check students' comprehension of the phrase: *I don't know.* Point to a relatively obscure object in the classroom. Ask: *What is it?* Shrug your shoulders and say: *I don't know.* Point out that this phrase is an extremely useful expression that can be used when an answer is not known. Demonstrate the usefulness of the phrase by circulating around the classroom and asking students to name additional obscure objects. Elicit the response: *I don't know.* Encourage students to use body language when they respond to your questions.

continued

6. Drill. Call out a variety of items and have students respond by clarifying in a positive format:

   T: *airplane*
   C: *Is it an airplane?*
   Continue: *star/UFO/jet/helicopter*

7. Drill:

   T: *Is it an airplane?*
   C: *No, it isn't an airplane.*
   Continue: *star/UFO/jet/helicopter*

8. Silent Reading. Have students uncover the text and read the first conversation silently.

9. Paired Reading. Divide the class into pairs and have them read the conversation together. Then have students reverse roles.

10. Ask questions about objects in the classroom.

    T: *Is it (a pen)?*
    S: *No, it isn't./Yes, it is./No, it isn't. It's (a book)./I don't know.*
    T: *What is it?*
    S: *It's (a book)./I don't know.*

11. Pair Work. Have students ask and answer questions as in the step above.

■ CONVERSATION 2 (Al/Bill)

1. Have students look at the picture once again.

2. Remind students to cover the conversation.

3. Play the recording. Play it again, pausing for students to repeat after each line, chorally and individually.

4. Demonstrate the meaning of the phrase: *It's open./It's not open.* by opening and closing the classroom door.

5. Silent Reading.

6. Paired Reading.

7. Drill:

   T: *radios*
   C: *Are they radios?*
   Continue: *CD players/computers/cassette players/VCRs*

8. Drill:

   T: *Are they radios?*
   C: *No, they aren't radios.*
   Continue: *CD players/computers/cassette players/VCRs*

■ PICTURES (21–40)

1. Have students repeat the numbers 21–40 after you.

2. Write the numbers on the board, point to a few, and have the class call out the numbers chorally.

3. Ask individual students: *What is it?* Point to a number on the board. Elicit the correct response. (*It's twenty-seven.*, etc.)

4. Pair Work. Have students work in pairs as above.

5. Pictures 21–25
   Ask questions:

   T: *21—Is it a picture?*
   S: *Yes, it is./No, it isn't.*
   T: *What is it?*
   S: *It's a picture.*

6. Pair Work. Have students work in pairs as above.

7. Pictures 26–30
   Ask questions:

   T: *26—Is it an airplane?*
   S: *Yes, it is./No, it isn't.*
   T: *What is it?*
   S: *It's an airplane.*

   Check that students use *an* before appropriate items.

8. Pictures 31–35
   Use the same steps as above, using *Are they…? What are they?*

9. Pictures 36–40
   Use the same steps as above, using *Are they…? What are they?*

10. Pair Work. Have students work in pairs, using all of the pictures on the page.

    S1: *37.*
    S2: *What are they?*
    S1: *They're watches.*

A. Game: What's number 22?

1. Introduce the concept of the game by playing a slightly different version to the one in the Student Book. Have students work in small groups. Ask individual students to take turns thinking of a singular object (21–30). Have the other students in the group ask questions until they guess the identity of the object.

continued

A Game: What's number 22?

Study the numbers and the pictures for two minutes.

Student A, open the book. Student B, close the book.

A: What's number 22?
B: It's a fork.
A: What's number 36?
B: They're dictionaries./I don't know.

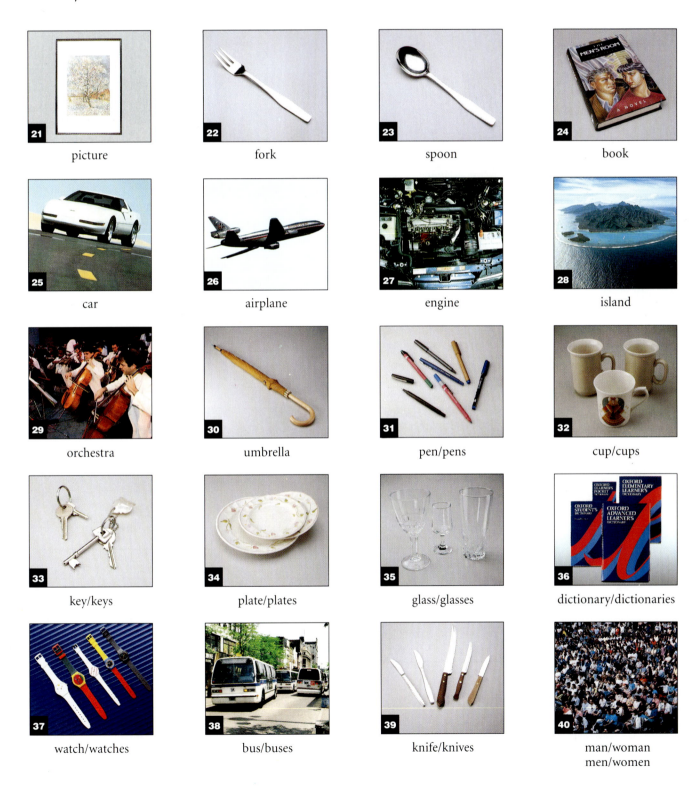

21 picture
22 fork
23 spoon
24 book
25 car
26 airplane
27 engine
28 island
29 orchestra
30 umbrella
31 pen/pens
32 cup/cups
33 key/keys
34 plate/plates
35 glass/glasses
36 dictionary/dictionaries
37 watch/watches
38 bus/buses
39 knife/knives
40 man/woman
men/women

B What is it?/What are they?

Write sentences using these words:

computer, radio, CD player, cassette player, speaker, TV, VCR

It's a computer./They're computers.

C Game: Bingo!

1. Write nine numbers (between 21 and 99) in Box 1. Play Bingo! with your teacher.

2. Write nine numbers (between 21 and 99) in Box 2. Play Bingo! with your partner.

Box 1		

Box 2		

S1: *Is it a cup?*
S2: *No, it isn't.*
S3: *Is it a fork?*
S2: *Yes, it is.*

Repeat the game with the remainder of the pictures on the page.

2. Read the directions to the game and the model dialogue out loud to the class. Explain that this is a memory game and that they should memorize the number of each item. Give students two minutes to study the numbers and pictures.

3. Pair Work. Have students play the game in pairs; one student keeps the book open and the other closes it. After students have practiced all of the items, have them switch roles.

4. Expansion. Devise another type of memory game by putting a collection of objects on a desk. Ask students to examine all of the items and then cover them with a cloth or put them elsewhere. Encourage students to tell you the names of all the objects. Write the names of the objects on the board. Students can also prepare their own memory games to play in class on a later date.

■ PLURAL SPELLINGS

1. Direct students' attention to the pictures once again. Point out that some of the words on the page are the result of some special spelling rules. Explain the following rules:

   • When a singular noun ends with *f* or *fe*, change the *f* or *fe* to *v* and add *es* to make the plural form. Show students 39. knife/knives.
   • When a singular noun ends with *y* and is preceded by a consonant, change the *y* to *i* and add *es* to make the plural form. Show students 36. dictionary/dictionaries.
   • Some singular nouns have irregular plural forms. Memorization is necessary: Show students 40. man/men and woman/women.

2. Comprehension Dictation. Dictate ten of the plural nouns to the class. Check answers on the board.

■ PRONUNCIATION

1. Model the correct pronunciation of the plural nouns, having students repeat after you.

2. Point out the different *s* endings. Compare the sound of *cups* [s], *keys* [z], and *watches* [ɪz].

3. Aural Discrimination. Put three columns on the board, labeling them 1, 2, and 3. Point to 1 and say: [s]. Point to 2 and say: [z]. Point to 3 and say: [ɪz]. Then say a variety of plural nouns and have students respond with the appropriate column number. Write the words in the correct column as students answer.

B. What is it?/What are they?

1. Have students examine the illustration. Encourage them to ask questions about any of the items.

2. Point to an item in the illustration. Say: *It's a VCR.* Have students repeat after you chorally. Point to two items and say: *They're VCRs.* Again have students repeat after you chorally.

3. Have students write sentences using the listed words.

4. Pair Work. Have students exchange papers and check answers.

C. Game: Bingo!

1. Have students write nine numbers of their choice (between 21 and 99) in Box 1.

2. Play a game of Bingo with the class by calling out numbers at random. Have students cross off the numbers that match the ones on their card. The first student to cross off all the numbers is the winner.

3. Pair Work. Have students write nine numbers of their choice (between 21 and 99) in Box 2.

4. Have students work in pairs, making sure that each partner does not see the other's card. Have each student call out numbers in turn. The student who crosses off all their numbers first is the winner.

■ WORKBOOK

The Workbook can be done for homework and checked in class. If you wish to use it in class, Exercises B, C, D, and E can be done as oral pair work. Students can write their answers, switch roles, and redo the exercises.

4 Names and addresses

> **Teaching points**
> Personal information: Names, addresses, telephone numbers
> Possessive adjectives (singular only)
> *Who's that?*
> *What's my/your/his/her/name?/address?/phone number?*
> *My/Your/His/Her name's (Sullivan).*
> *I'm/You're/He's/She's (Sullivan).*
> *What's my/your/his/her/first/last name?*
> *Where's he from?*
> *My name isn't (Sullivan).*
> Numbers: 100–999
> The Alphabet: Spelling
> Listening for specific information (personal details)
> Reading: Extracting relevant information from diagrams: (marathon program)
>
> **Expressions**
> *Sorry.*
> *That's OK.*
> *…, right?*
> *Well, anyway…*
> *What?* (informal *Excuse me?*)
> *first/last name*
>
> **Active vocabulary**
> address/alphabet/can/come/do/fantastic/game/go/help/her/here/his/how/last/locker room/lost/name/now/number/people/phone number/sorry/spell/to/who/with/your
>
> **Passive vocabulary**
> about/answer (v.)/ask/chart/marathon/on/program/question (n.)/runner/say/their/these
>
> **Abbreviations**
> OK/ID/VW/PM/USA/FBI/IBM/UFO
>
> **Audiovisual aids**
> Cassette/CD
> **Expansion:** sports pages from local newspaper

■ ORAL INTRODUCTION

Say: *My name's (Susan). What's your name?* Ask several students, getting them to respond with: *My name's (Yuki).*, etc. Say: *His name's (Angelo). Her name's (Gina).* Ask: *What's his name? What's her name?* about several students.

■ CONVERSATION 1 (Man, Woman)

1. Have students look at the picture. Make sure that students are covering the conversation in their books. Encourage students to talk about the action going on in the picture. Talk about the players.

2. Play the recording. Play it again, pausing for students to repeat, chorally and individually.

3. Ask students the following questions: *What's his name? Is he number 2? Is he number 11? What's his number? Is he from New York? Is he from San Diego? Where's he from? Is he good?*

Culture note: The All Star Baseball Game is an annual event in the United States in which the best players from the two baseball leagues—the National League and the American League—compete. Fans of the different teams vote for their favorite players. The game takes place midway through the regular baseball season.

4. Silent Reading.

5. Paired Reading.

6. Role Play. In pairs, have students role play the conversation. Encourage students to substitute other names, numbers, and teams.

4 Names and addresses

Man: Who's that? He's number seven.
Woman: His name's Sullivan.
Man: What's his first name?
Woman: Kevin.
Man: Where's he from?
Woman: Philadelphia. He's fantastic!

A What's your name?

Listen to the conversations. Look at the picture on page 13. Write A, E, I, O, U, and Y.

A: Come here, Sullivan.
E: My name isn't Sullivan.
A: Sorry.
E: That's OK.
A: What *is* your name?
E: Sandberg. I'm Josh Sandberg.
A: Oh. Your number is seven, right?
E: No, it isn't. I'm number two. Sullivan is number seven.
A: Well, anyway, go to the locker room.
E: What?
A: Go to the locker room. You're out of the game. Go now!

I: Can you help me? I'm lost.
O: What's your name?
I: Joey.
O: What's your last name, Joey?
I: Maggio.
O: And what's your address?
I: 32 Fuller Road, Fort Worth, Texas 76101.
O: What's your phone number?
I: 650-4893.

U: What's your name?
Y: Reid.
U: Spell it, please.
Y: R-E-I-D.
U: First name?
Y: Sam.
U: OK, Mr. Reid. Come with me.

B Numbers

100 — a hundred/one hundred
200 — two hundred
305 — three hundred (and) five

Number: **650**
Say: six hundred (and) fifty/six-fifty.

Telephone number: **650-4893**
Say: six-five-oh—four-eight—nine-three.

1. Say these numbers:

   100   104   212   327   439
   561   655   792   848   910

2. Say these telephone numbers:

   332-1010   596-7429   802-4768

C The alphabet

1. Say:

   A H J K
   B C D E G P T V Z
   F L M N S X
   I Y
   U W Q
   O R

2. Say:

   OK   ID   VW   PM   USA   FBI   IBM   UFO

D Marathon

Look at number 219 on the marathon program.

**INTERNATIONAL WOMEN'S MARATHON
PITTSBURGH, PENNSYLVANIA
APRIL 16TH – 10:00 AM**

THE ENTRANTS ARE:

#	Name	Country
#125	Joan Benito	(U.S.)
#104	Olga Dejnak	(Russia)
#363	Annie Flandreau	(France)
#219	Grace Fong	(Hong Kong)
#77	Kimiko Ito	(Japan)
#250	Bianca López	(Venezuela)
#91	Lucia Pavino	(Italy)
#184	Alison Gilbert	(Great Britain)

A: Who's that? She's number 219.
B: Her name's Fong.
A: How do you spell it?
B: F-O-N-G.
A: What's her first name?
B: Grace.
A: Where's she from?
B: Hong Kong.

Ask and answer questions about the other runners in the marathon.

A. What's your name?

1. Have students look at the picture on page 13. Explain that they are going to hear three conversations on the recording. Have them match AE, IO, and UY to indicate the speakers in the picture.

2. Play all of the conversations on the recording.

3. Play the tape/CD again and check answers.

■ CONVERSATION 1 (A, E)

1. Ask the question: *What number is Sullivan?* Play the first conversation again and check students' answers.

2. Play the tape/CD again, pausing for students to repeat, chorally and individually. Note the stress on What *is* your name? Have students repeat after you, emphasizing the word *is*.

3. Demonstrate the meaning of the words *come* and *go*. Say: *Come here. Go to the door. Go to the window.* Have students follow your instructions.

4. Demonstrate the meaning of *sorry* by pretending to confuse students' names. Call students by the wrong names and apologize.

5. Drill:

   T: *your*
   C: *What's your number?*
   Continue: *his/my/her/your/her*

6. Silent Reading.

7. Questions: *Is his name Sullivan? Is his name Torrez? What is his name? Is he number 11? Is he number 7? What is his number? Is he sorry? Is it OK?*

8. Paired Reading.

9. Role Play. Have students role play the conversation, substituting other names and numbers. Write the names of some baseball players on the board (for example, from the U.S.: Clemens, Winfield, Clark, Wilson, Boggs, Strawberry, etc.). Variation: If possible, bring in the local newspaper's sports page (if baseball is in season) and encourage students to copy down players' names to use in their role plays.

10. Pair Work. Have students give instructions with *come* and *go* as demonstrated in Step 3 above.

    Culture note: Explain the role of the umpire in a baseball game. Umpires have the authority to rule on plays and to remove players from the game who break rules or misbehave. Players and managers have to respect umpires' decisions and not argue with them. In the situation here, the umpire is removing the pitcher (#2, Sandberg) from the game for throwing a "spitball." Pitchers are not allowed to put spit or other substances (for example, oil, hair cream, etc.) on the baseball to help them throw it. If a pitcher does this (as Sandberg does here) and the umpire catches him (the umpire finds something on the baseball), he can tell the pitcher to leave the game. In this case, a new pitcher will have to come into the game to replace Sandberg.

■ CONVERSATION 2 (I, O)

1. Ask the question: *What's his telephone number?* Play the conversation again and check students' answers.

2. Play the tape/CD again, pausing for students to repeat, chorally and individually.

3. Drill:

   T: *name*
   C: *What's your name?*
   Continue: *first name/last name/address/telephone number*

4. Drill:

   T: *name*
   C: *What's your name?*
   T: *his*
   C: *What's his name?*
   T: *address*
   C: *What's his address?*
   Continue: *her/telephone number/number/my/last name/your*

5. Silent Reading.

6. Paired Reading.

7. Role Play. Have students role play the conversation, substituting their own names, addresses, and telephone numbers.

■ CONVERSATION 3 (U, Y)

1. Ask the question: *What is his name?* Play the conversation again and check students' answers.

2. Play the tape/CD again, pausing for students to repeat, chorally and individually.

continued

3. Silent Reading.
4. Questions. Ask: *What's his first name? Spell Reid.*
5. Ask students questions about themselves.
6. Paired Reading.
7. Role Play. Have students role play, substituting their own names, addresses, and telephone numbers.

B. Numbers

1. Silent Reading.
2. Ask volunteers to say the numbers. Check: *two hundred* and not *two hundreds*.
3. Write more three-figure numbers on the board, indicate individuals, and get them to say the numbers.
4. Ask students to say the telephone numbers.
5. Comprehension Dictation. Dictate the following numbers: *817/294/500/190/819/340/614/757/727.* Then have students put them in numerical order.

C. The alphabet

1. Have students repeat the letters of the alphabet, one group of letters at a time. Write some on the board and ask volunteers to say them.
2. Have students repeat the groups of abbreviations.
3. Ask individual students to spell their names.
4. Call out these letters and ask students to write them down: *a/i/y/e/o/b/e/c/i/a/u/w/v/p/b.* Check students' answers.

D. Marathon

1. Model the dialogue. Model it again with a student, switching roles.
2. Pair Work. Have students work on the dialogue and substitutions from the program, switching roles.
3. Ask volunteers to demonstrate the dialogue in front of the class.

E. Chart

1. Pair Work. Have students ask and answer questions about the people listed on the chart.
2. Have students complete the information about themselves.
3. Have students interview their partner, filling in the information on the chart.

F. Three people

1. Review the format for this type of exercise (See Unit 2, Exercise B, Four conversations).
2. Play each conversation twice. Have students fill in the missing information after the second listening.
3. Pair Work. Have students compare their answers by asking and answering in pairs. Check the answers with a few questions.
4. Play the conversations once again. Have students check their answers.
5. Game: Alphabetical order. Have students form a line around the class in strict alphabetical order *(Maria* before *Marie).* In order for students to accomplish this, they must circulate and ask other students to spell their first names. The game can be repeated using last names.

■ WORKBOOK

The Workbook can be done for homework and checked in class. Exercise A is reading an authentic text for specific information. Explain that you do not need to understand all of the written information in order to complete the exercise. Do not spend time explaining vocabulary that is not needed for the exercise. If you wish to use the Workbook in class, Exercises C and D can be done as oral pair work. Exercise G is an oral exercise and should be done in class. Exercise H is a matching exercise, designed to focus on the letters of the alphabet used in abbreviations (listed in Exercise G). Do not explain meanings.

E Chart

	Name		Address	Phone number
	Last	**First**		
1.	Novak	Sarah	350 Bridge Street Lincoln, Nebraska 68501	402-677-3288
2.	Knight	Michael	17 North Road Madison, Wisconsin 53701	608-534-9695
3.	(you)			
4.	(your partner)			

her / his / your

What's…last name? What's…first name?
What's…address? What's…phone number?

1. Ask and answer questions about Ms. Novak and Mr. Knight.
2. Write your name, address, and telephone number.
3. Talk to your partner. Write his/her name, address, and phone number.

F Three people

	1	2	3
Last name			
First name			
Address			
Phone number			

1. Listen to the three people. Write their names, addresses, and phone numbers.
2. Ask and answer questions about the people.

5 Lambert and Stacey

1.
Stacey: Hello?
1st Man: Is tonight OK?
Stacey: Yes.
1st Man: The Main Street parking garage, then. 11:00. With the painting.
Stacey: And the diamonds?
1st Man: Yeah, yeah. They're here.

2.
Stacey: What time is it?
Lambert: Eleven-fifteen. They're late.
Stacey: Well, we're on time. Listen. What's that?
Lambert: It's a car. Is it their car?
Stacey: Yeah, it is. Come on.

3.
1st Man: OK, where's the painting?
Stacey: The Picasso?
1st Man: Yeah, the Picasso. Where is it?
Stacey: It's here, in the briefcase. Where are the diamonds?
1st Man: They're in the bag.
Lambert: Where's the bag?
2nd Man: It's in our car.
Stacey: Get it.

4.
Lambert: OK, hands on the car! I'm Lambert, she's Stacey. We're detectives.
1st Man: You're detectives?
Lambert: City Police.
2nd Man: Oh, this is great! We're detectives, too. FBI.
Stacey: Oh yeah? Where are your identity cards?
1st Man: Our ID cards? They're in the car.
Stacey: Get their IDs, Lambert.
Lambert: Oh no! It's true! They *are* detectives!

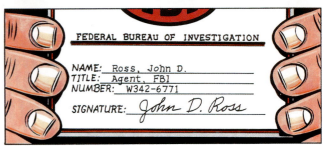

5 Lambert and Stacey

Teaching points
Verb *to be*; plurals—1st, 2nd, 3rd person
We/you/they are (detectives); Questions/Negatives
Possessive adjectives—plural *our/your/their*
Time: *What time is it?*
It's six o'clock/ten-forty/eleven-thirty.
Where is it?/are they?
It's in…/They're in…
What's that?
late
first (1st)/second (2nd)
Simple letter format:
Dear…/Regards
Reading: From a handwritten letter. Extracting information from a guest registration card

Expressions
Hello? (on the phone)
…, then
on time
Come on.
Oh, this is great!
Dear…,/Regards
Really?

Active vocabulary
bag/briefcase/detective/diamond/FBI/get/hand/hotel/ID/identity card/in/late/o'clock/on/our/painting/parking garage/room/same/student/suitcase/teacher/their/time/tonight/too (also)/true/we/what time

Passive vocabulary
another/at/business/complete (v.)/continue/couple/friend/happy/have/home/know/meet/new/of/or/registration card/form/role play/this

Incidental vocabulary
Federal Bureau of Investigation

Audiovisual aids
Cassette/CD
Realia: single/plural objects
Clock with movable hands
Reproduction of a Picasso painting
Note: The initial emphasis of the four dialogues is listening. Intensive practice of each dialogue follows. With false beginners you will be able to ask more interesting questions as you play the dialogues.

■ ORAL INTRODUCTION

1. Put a pen in a bag. Say: *Where is it? It's in the bag.* Take it out. Put two pens in the bag. Say: *Where are they? They're in the bag.* Continue putting objects into bags, desks, books, etc., and asking individuals: *Where is it? Where are they?*

2. Pair Work. Get students to do the same in pairs.

3. Hold up two pens, say: *They're pens.* Bring out two students, say: *They're students.* Ask: *Are they teachers? Are they men? What are they? Are they in a car? Where are they?* Point to other pairs/groups of students. Ask the same questions.

4. Have the students stand up. Say: *We're in the classroom. We aren't in (Mexico). We're in (Japan).* Ask the class (to elicit answer with *you*): *Are we in an airplane? Where are we? Are we in (Mexico)? Where are we?* Ask the students standing with you the same questions (to elicit answers with *we*).

■ CONVERSATION 1

1. Focus attention on the top picture. Check that the text is covered.

2. Play the recording.

3. Ask: *What is a painting?* Draw a "painting" with a frame around it on the board. Ask: *What are diamonds?* Draw a diamond shape on the board.

■ CONVERSATION 2

1. Focus attention on the picture. Check that the text is covered.

2. Play the recording.

3. Point to your watch and ask: *What time is it?* Play the conversation again. Explain *late* and *early*. Write on the board: *10:55/11:00/11:15*. Say: *11:00 is on time. 10:55 is early. 11:15 is late.*

4. Demonstrate: *Listen.* Put your hand behind your ear as though you just heard a noise. Have students repeat the gesture.

continued

■ CONVERSATIONS 3 AND 4

1. Focus attention on the pictures. Check that the text is covered.
2. Play the tape/CD for both conversations.
3. Explain: *Picasso*. (If possible, show students a reproduction of a Picasso painting.)
4. Ask: *Are the men detectives? Are the women detectives?*

■ INTENSIVE PRACTICE: CONVERSATION 1

1. Play the tape/CD again, pausing for selective repetition. *Hello?/Is tonight OK?/With the painting./And the diamonds?/They're here.*
2. Silent Reading.
3. Paired Reading.

■ INTENSIVE PRACTICE: CONVERSATION 2

1. Play the tape/CD again, pausing for students to repeat, chorally and individually.
2. Silent Reading.
3. Point out: *They're late./Is it their car?* Write on the board: *they're/their*. Have students repeat. Show that the pronunciation of the two words is the same.
4. Drill:

    T: *they*
    C: *They're late.*
    Continue: *I/he/we/you/she/they/John/Fumiko and Kenji.*

5. Paired Reading.

■ INTENSIVE PRACTICE: CONVERSATION 3

1. Play the tape/CD again, pausing for students to repeat, chorally and individually.
2. Drill:

    T: *painting*
    C: *Where's the painting?*
    T: *diamonds*
    C: *Where are the diamonds?*
    Continue: *pen/books/dictionary/forks/spoons*

3. Silent Reading.
4. Paired Reading.
5. Questions. Ask: *Where is the painting? Is it a Picasso? Are the diamonds in the briefcase? Where are they? Where is the bag?*

6. Total Physical Response. Give students the following directions: *Get the pen. Get her book. Get his bag.*, etc. Make sure that students follow the instructions precisely. They do not need to speak. Get them to do the same in pairs.
7. Drill:

    T: *my*
    C: *It's my car.*
    Continue: *his/their/our/her/your/my*

■ INTENSIVE PRACTICE: CONVERSATION 4

1. Play the tape/CD again, pausing for selective repetition. *We're detectives./You're detectives./We're detectives, too./They are detectives.* Note the changing stress/intonation. Make sure that students imitate it.
2. Silent Reading.
3. Have students examine the FBI identity card. Ask them to study it for a moment.
4. Pair Work. Have students ask and answer questions about the card: *What is his last name? What's his job? What's his number?*, etc.

■ ROLE PLAY

1. Play all four conversations again.
2. Put students into groups of four. Have them role play the entire conversation with books closed.

A. What time is it?

Note: Time is only taught in the *ten-twenty, ten-forty* style at this time. It is easier for students to generate these phrases than *twenty after ten, twenty to eleven* which are covered in *Main Street, Student Book 2*.

1. Focus attention on the examples. Ask individuals to tell you the time on each of the clocks.
2. Using a clock with movable hands, ask students to tell you the time. Go around the entire class so that everyone has a turn.
3. Pair Work. Have students ask and answer about clocks 1–13.

A What time is it?

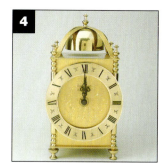

A: Look at number 1. What time is it?
B: It's six o'clock.

A: Look at number 2. What time is it?
B: It's ten-forty.

A: Look at number 3. What time is it?
B: It's eleven-thirty.

Continue.

B Questions

Ask and answer questions.

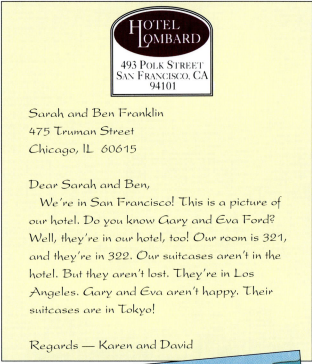

HOTEL LOMBARD
493 POLK STREET
SAN FRANCISCO, CA
94101

Sarah and Ben Franklin
475 Truman Street
Chicago, IL 60615

Dear Sarah and Ben,
  We're in San Francisco! This is a picture of our hotel. Do you know Gary and Eva Ford? Well, they're in our hotel, too! Our room is 321, and they're in 322. Our suitcases aren't in the hotel. But they aren't lost. They're in Los Angeles. Gary and Eva aren't happy. Their suitcases are in Tokyo!

Regards — Karen and David

1. Are Karen and David in Los Angeles?
2. Where are they?
3. What's their room number?
4. Are their suitcases in San Francisco?
5. Are their suitcases lost?
6. Where are they?
7. Where are Gary and Eva?
8. What's their room number?
9. Where are their suitcases?
10. Are Sarah and Ben in the same hotel?
11. What's their address?

C New friends

Karen and David Kennedy meet another couple at their hotel. Look at their registration cards. Complete their conversation.

HOTEL LOMBARD REGISTRATION FORM
493 POLK STREET • SAN FRANCISCO • CALIFORNIA 94101
NAME: David and Karen Kennedy
BUSINESS: teachers
HOME ADDRESS: 471 Truman Street
Chicago, Illinois 60615
ROOM NUMBER: 321

HOTEL LOMBARD REGISTRATION FORM
493 POLK STREET • SAN FRANCISCO • CALIFORNIA 94101
NAME: Anne and Peter Quinn
BUSINESS: teachers
HOME ADDRESS: 1413 Harding Road
Concord, New Hampshire 03301
ROOM NUMBER: 327

Anne: Hello. _____ Peter and Anne Quinn.
Karen: Hi. Our _____ David and Karen Kennedy. _____ students?
Peter: No, _____. We _____.
Karen: You're teachers? Really? We _____ teachers too.
David: Where _____ from?
Anne: _____. And you? Where _____?
David: _____.
Anne: What room _____ in? _____ in _____.
Karen: _____.

D Role play

Student A, you're Karen or David Kennedy. Student B, you're Peter or Anne Quinn. Look at your registration cards. Have a conversation.

Read *Story for Pleasure: Air Traffic Control* on page 72.

B. Questions

1. Focus students' attention on the letter.
2. Silent Reading.
3. Pair Work. Have students ask and answer the questions.
4. Read the letter aloud. Ask the questions to individuals as a check.

C. New friends

1. Focus attention on the guest registration card.
2. Silent Reading.
3. Questions. Ask: *What's their last name? What are their first names? Are they students? What are they? Where are they from? What's their address? What's their room number?*
4. Pair Work. Have students ask similar questions about the registration card.
5. Open Conversation. Have students complete the conversation orally in pairs. Or have students do this as a written assignment.

D. Role play

In pairs, have students role play a conversation between two of the characters.

■ WORKBOOK

The Workbook can be done for homework and checked in class. If you wish to use it in class, Exercises A, B, and E can be done as oral pair work.

See *Story for Pleasure: Air Traffic Control* on page 72.

The train to Chicago

Teaching points
this/that/these/those
here/there
How much is that?
($12.40) each./That's ($24.80).
Prepositions: *on* (track 3) *next to* (the door)
When's the (next train)?
Listening for specific information (timetables)
Reading for specific information (tickets, timetables)

Grammar note
In this unit *How much?* is used for price, not quantity.
Demonstratives *(this, that, these, those)*: Although it is useful to introduce the concept with distance *(this/these* for near things, *that/those* for further away things), you could add the concept of variation. Alternate between them for variety. *This is a pen and that's a pencil.* (Even though they are at the same distance from the speaker.)

Expressions
Yes?
one way
round trip
Excuse me. (to get someone's attention)
Are these seats taken?
in (the wrong) line
on track 12
next to the exit

Active vocabulary
but/cafeteria/door/each/exit/for/free (available)/gift shop/how much/line/newsstand/next (adj.)/next to/office/rest room/seat/these/this/those/ticket/track/train/train station/video arcade/when/window/wrong

Passive vocabulary
AM/announcement/departure/leave/place (n.)/price

Audiovisual aids
Cassette/CD
Expansion: Authentic timetables and/or fares lists
Realia: Classroom objects (for introduction)

■ ORAL INTRODUCTION

Briefly demonstrate *this, that, these, those* using classroom objects or optional realia. Point at objects at a distance for *that* and *those*. In addition, use the words *here* and *there* to indicate distance.
It's here. This is a door.
They're here. These are chairs.
It's there. That's a table.
They're there. Those are windows.

A. Where's the newsstand?

1. Have students examine the picture of the train station. Ask questions to elicit: *It's next to....*

   T: *Where's the cafeteria?*
   S: *It's next to tracks 1 and 2.*

   Do not bother to teach the multitude of vocabulary items illustrated on this page.

2. Play the recording. Play it again, pausing for students to repeat, chorally and individually.

3. Pair Work. Have students work together to ask and answer questions about the location of places in the illustration.

4. Expansion. Place several objects in a row on your desk. Ask individuals questions about the placement of the objects: *Where's the pen? Where are the erasers?* Ask volunteers for the answers.

6 The train to Chicago

A Where's the newsstand?

Look at the picture of the train station. Ask and answer questions about places in the train station.

A: Where's the newsstand?
B: It's next to tracks 5 and 6/the gift shop.
A: Where are the rest rooms?
B: They're next to tracks 5 and 6/tracks 7 and 8.

19

1.
Woman: Yes?
Diana: Two tickets to Chicago, please.
Woman: You're in the wrong line. This is the line for St. Louis.
Diana: Where's the line for Chicago?
Woman: That's it over there. Window number 4.

2.
Diana: Two tickets to Chicago, please.
Man: One way or round trip?
Diana: Round trip. How much is that?
Man: $12.40 each. That's $24.80.
Diana: When's the next train?
Man: 3:25.

3.
Philip: Excuse me, is this the train to Chicago?
Man: No, it isn't. That's the Chicago train over there.
Philip: Where?
Man: On track 12.
Philip: Thank you.
Man: You're welcome.

4.
Diana: Excuse me, are these seats taken?
Woman: Yes, they are. But those seats are free.
Diana: Where?
Woman: Over there. Next to the door.
Diana: Thank you.

■ CONVERSATION 1 (Woman, Diana)

1. Have students examine the illustration above the conversation. Check that the text is covered.
2. Ask students to speculate what is happening. Ask: *What is she buying? Where is she going?*
3. Play the recording. Play it again, pausing for students to repeat, chorally and individually.
4. Silent Reading.
5. Paired Reading.

■ CONVERSATION 2 (Diana, Man)

1. Have students examine the illustration above the conversation. Check that the text is covered.
2. Explain: *one way* and *round trip*.
3. Play the recording. Play it again, pausing for students to repeat, chorally and individually.
4. Silent Reading.
5. Paired Reading.

■ CONVERSATION 3 (Philip, Man)

1. Have students examine the illustration above the conversation. Check that the text is covered.
2. Play the recording. Play it again, pausing for students to repeat, chorally and individually.
3. Drill:

    T: *The Chicago train is here.*
    C: *This is the Chicago train.*
    T: *The St. Louis train is over there.*
    C: *That's the St. Louis train.*
    Pronunciation Note: The proper pronunciation of the city, St. Louis, is St. "Lewis." Students may be more familiar with the pronunciation "Louie." The latter pronunciation is only a nickname used in a few popular songs.
    Continue: *The Philadelphia train is here. The Boston train is over there. The Miami train is here. The Dallas train is over there.*

4. Silent Reading.
5. Paired Reading.

■ CONVERSATION 4 (Diana, Woman)

1. Have students examine the illustration above the conversation. Check that the text is covered.
2. Play the recording. Play it again, pausing for students to repeat, chorally and individually.
3. Drill:

    T: *The seats are here.*
    C: *These seats?*
    T: *The seats are over there.*
    C: *Those seats?*
    Continue: *The tables are here. The tables are over there. The chairs are over there. The chairs are here.*

4. Silent Reading.
5. Paired Reading.

■ CONVERSATION 5 (Philip, Diana)

1. Have students examine the illustration above the conversation. Check that the text is covered.

2. Play the recording. Play it again, pausing for students to repeat, chorally and individually.

3. Drill:

   T: *My suitcases aren't here.*
   C: *These aren't my suitcases.*
   T: *My pens aren't there.*
   C: *Those aren't my pens.*
   Continue: *My suitcases aren't there. My pens aren't here. My books aren't there. My sandwiches aren't here.*

4. Silent Reading.

5. Paired Reading.

6. Play all five dialogues again.

B. How much is...?

1. Reading for specific information. Have students examine the fare guide.

2. Model the dialogue. Have students repeat after you.

3. Ask students to look at the guide and find the following information: *How much does it cost to go to Louisville, Kentucky? Does this train go to New Orleans? How much is a ticket to Detroit? Does the train go to New York?*, etc.

4. Pair Work. Have students ask and answer questions about the fare guide.

5. Expansion. Distribute real train and/or bus fare guides to the class. Ask additional questions. Have the class ask and answer similar questions.

C. Departures

1. Have students examine the departure board.

2. Model the dialogue. Have students repeat after you.

3. Brainstorm other ways to ask the time: *What time does the train for Kansas City leave? When does the train for Kansas City depart? When's the train for Kansas City leaving?*

4. Pair Work. Have students ask and answer questions based on the departure board.

5. Role Play. Encourage students to combine the dialogues they have just practiced (about prices and train departure times), substituting various prices and times.

D. Announcements

1. Have students examine the chart. Play the announcements on the tape/CD twice, getting students to fill in the information on the second listening.

2. Pair Work. Have students exchange books to check answers.

3. Check answers by asking questions. Play the tape/CD again, if necessary.

■ ORAL PRACTICE

1. Review *this/that* again. Put several objects on your desk. Ask a few students: *What's this?* Make sure that they reply: *That's a (book).* Follow the same procedure with plurals. Ask: *What are these?* Elicit: *Those are (pens).*

2. Pair Work. Distribute some objects to students. Demonstrate that every pair now has some near objects and some far objects to ask about: *What's this? What's that? What are these? What are those?* Have students ask and answer about the objects.

3. For variety, put two objects near you on your desk. Say: *This is a pen, and that's a book.* Put two groups of objects near you and say: *These are pens and those are books.*

4. Expansion. Game: I spy. Have students play a guessing game. Ask one student to think of an object and tell the class the first letter of the object (a word with *b*). The class asks questions until they can guess the object. *Is it a book? Is it a ball? Is it a bag?* The game (which can be played at any time in the series) is very limited due to the lack of vocabulary, but it can be used as a way of getting students to use the Vocabulary Index at the back of their books. Limit the game to words in Units 1 to 6.

5. Expansion. Use authentic timetables as the basis for role plays during the lesson. If possible, distribute a variety of different timetables. This will involve reading for specific information as part of the role play activity.

■ WORKBOOK

The Workbook can be done for homework and checked in class. If you wish to use it in class, Exercises D to G can be done as oral pair work.

5.
Philip: Well, we're here. This is Chicago.
Diana: Philip! Those aren't our suitcases!
Philip: They aren't?
Diana: No. These are our suitcases, over here.

B How much is…?

Ask and answer questions about the prices of one-way tickets.

AM-RAIL EXPRESS ONE-WAY FARES

Chicago —	
Milwaukee, Wisconsin	$ 10.25
Detroit, Michigan	30.00
St. Louis, Missouri	30.50
Louisville, Kentucky	35.40
Nashville, Tennessee	53.20
Memphis, Tennessee	54.60
New Orleans, Louisiana	85.00
Houston, Texas	100.95
Orlando, Florida	126.55

A: How much is a one-way ticket to Houston?
B: That's $100.95.

C Departures

Ask and answer questions about departure times.

TRAIN FOR	LEAVING AT	TRACK NO.
ST. LOUIS	5:40 PM	7
KANSAS CITY	5:55 PM	2
TORONTO	6:00 PM	3
NEW YORK	6:15 PM	
BOSTON	6:25 PM	
MILWAUKEE	6:30 PM	
NEW ORLEANS	6:45 PM	
TORONTO	6:50 PM	
ST. LOUIS	6:55 PM	

A: When's the train for Kansas City?
B: 5:55.

D Announcements

Listen. Write the times and the track numbers.

TRAIN FOR	LEAVING AT	TRACK NO.
NEW YORK	10:40 AM	4
TORONTO		
ST. LOUIS		
BOSTON		
NEW ORLEANS		

7 Space station

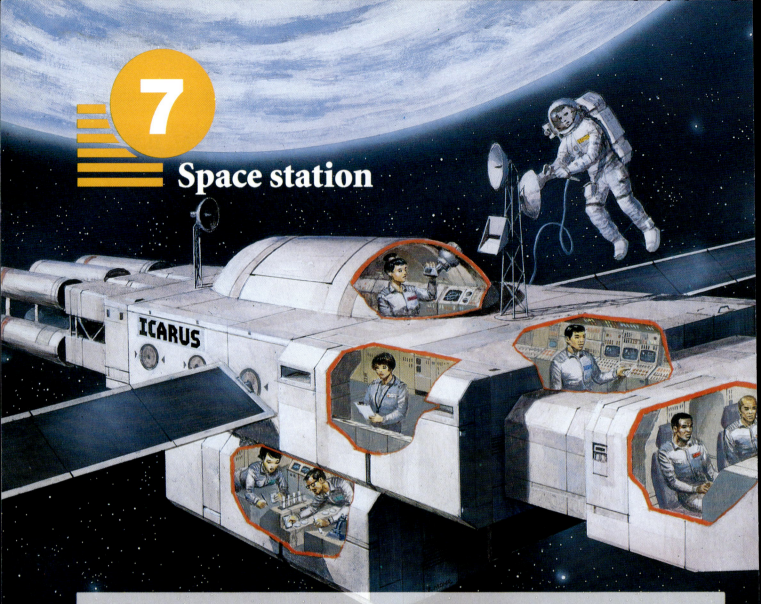

This is the crew of the new space station, *Icarus*. The crew members are from eight countries. *Icarus* is an international space station, and it's six thousand miles above the Earth.

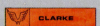 

Peter Clarke and Ivan Asimov are the pilots. Peter's American, and Ivan's Russian. Peter's thirty-two. He's from Los Angeles. Ivan's forty. He's from Moscow.

 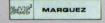

Yoko Suzuki and Antonio Márquez are the scientists on the space station. Yoko's thirty-one. She's Japanese, from Tokyo. Antonio's thirty-two. He's Spanish. He's from Madrid.

Marie Verne's twenty-nine, and she's the doctor on *Icarus*. Marie's French. She's from Paris.

Li Song is Chinese. He's the computer specialist. He's twenty-eight years old. He's from Beijing.

Mark Ballard is British, and he's the engineer. Mark's thirty-two. He's from London.

Cristina Cabral is Brazilian, from Rio de Janeiro. She's the astronomer on *Icarus*. She's twenty-nine years old.

Space station

Teaching points
Who is it?/Who are they?/Who's the doctor?/Who's from Los Angeles?
How old are you?/is she?
I'm twenty-one./I'm twenty-one years old.
What's your job?/nationality?
What's her job?/nationality?
Nationalities:
Russian/French/Japanese/American/Spanish/Chinese/Brazilian/British
Jobs
Four-figure numbers (1,000)
a/the: She's a doctor./She's the doctor on the space station.
Reading for pleasure: The facts about space travel do not have to be taught.

Grammar note
The focus of the lesson is facts about people. Exercise C shows the use of the definite article *(the)* compared with the use of indefinite articles *(a/an)*. We believe that this is a difficult concept for some students, and explanation should be avoided. If it is avoided, most students will find themselves doing the exercise successfully, without even noticing the contrast between *a* and *the*.

Active vocabulary
astronomer/doctor/engineer/how old/job/nationality/old/pilot/right (correct)/scientist/specialist/year

Passive vocabulary
above/age/answer (n.)/crew/Earth/guess (v.)/hometown/international/interview (n.)/member/mile/reporter/space station/statement/word

Incidental vocabulary
dog/first/joint/moon/orbital/project/skylab/space shuttle/traveler

Audiovisual aids
This unit is not recorded.

■ **ORAL INTRODUCTION**

Pretend that you have forgotten students' names. Ask: *Who's that?* to elicit *It's (Maria). It's (Yoshi).*, etc. Ask students to test your memory of students' names by indicating various students and asking: *Who's that?*

■ **TEXT**

1. Have students look at the reading about the space station. Begin a discussion about names. Say: *John is an English name.* Write the following nationalities on the board: *Russian/French/Japanese/Spanish/Chinese.* Ask students to skim the reading passage to find names that match the nationalities. Give assistance, if necessary.

2. Silent Reading.

Unit 7   Teacher's Book ■ 22

A. Crew chart

1. Explain the chart on the top of the page. Have students complete the chart for the remaining crew members. Tell students that it is all right for them to refer back to the text to complete the chart.

2. Review vocabulary items by asking: *Are the crew from eight countries or six countries? Is the space station American? Is it international? Is the space station on Earth or is it above the Earth?* (Demonstrate the meaning of *above* by moving your hand from on top of your desk to above your desk.) *Is the space station six hundred miles above the Earth or six thousand miles above the Earth?* Write *6,000* in numbers on the board.

3. Ask students to examine the illustration carefully. Hold up your book and ask: *Who is the doctor?* Ask them to show you on the picture. Ask questions about the other characters and have students point out the *pilot, engineer, scientist, computer specialist,* and *astronomer.*

4. Have students repeat the occupation words after you, chorally and individually.

B. Questions

1. Pair Work. Have students ask and answer the questions.

2. Check answers by reviewing the questions with the class.

3. Ask additional questions: *Who is American? Who is Brazilian? Who is 28? Who is Chinese? Who is from Tokyo?,* etc. Allow students to look at their text in order to answer the questions.

C. Who's…?/Who are…?

1. Have students examine the illustration. Point out the crew members' badges. Indicate the two possibilities: *She's a doctor. She's the doctor on Icarus./They're scientists. They're the scientists on Icarus.* Avoid complex explanations about definite and indefinite articles at this point, but encourage students to use both forms if they feel comfortable with them.

2. Model the sample dialogue. Have students repeat after you, chorally and individually.

3. Note the contraction *who's* and the pronunciation of *who are (who're).* We do not write this contraction, even though we say it.

4. Pair Work. Have students ask and answer the questions.

5. Check answers by reviewing the questions with the class.

6. With school-age classes, ask questions about famous people.
   T: *Madonna. What's her job?*
   S: *She's a singer./She's a rock star.*

   Use currently famous living people: baseball players, tennis players, actors, actresses, rock singers, etc. Note: Don't say: *What's Madonna's job?* The possessive form is not taught until later in the book.

7. Ask: *What's my job?* to elicit *You're a teacher.* With adult classes, ask: *What's your/his/her/my job?* Encourage students to ask each other.

D. How old…?

1. Model the sample dialogue. Have students repeat after you, chorally and individually.

2. Pair Work. Have students ask and answer the questions.

3. Check answers by reviewing the questions with the class.

4. Ask questions to the class: *How old are you? How old is he? How old is she? How old am I?* Note: If using this book with school-age students, there will only be two answers from most classes. Keep this activity short. Be sensitive with adult classes and avoid embarrassing students.

5. Expansion. Ask questions about famous people. You will have to prepare before class and find out the current ages of the famous people you have selected. If you do this activity, you could tell the students the ages and then make the questions into a memory game. The following dates of birth will help if you cannot find out any current ages before the lesson: Bruce Springsteen 9/23/49; Yoko Ono 2/18/33; Queen Elizabeth II 4/21/26; Steven Spielberg 12/18/47.

A Crew chart

Complete the chart.

Name	Job	Age	Nationality	Hometown
Peter Clarke	pilot	32	American	Los Angeles
Ivan Asimov				
Marie Verne				
Mark Ballard				
Yoko Suzuki				
Antonio Márquez				
Li Song				
Cristina Cabral				

B Questions

Ask and answer questions about the crew members.

1. Who are the pilots?
2. Who's the astronomer?
3. Who's from Japan?
4. Who's from Paris?
5. Who are the scientists?
6. Who's Spanish?
7. Who's forty years old?
8. Who's the computer specialist?
9. Who's from Rio de Janeiro?
10. Who's thirty-one?

C Who's…?/Who are…?

Ask and answer questions about jobs.

A: Who's Marie Verne? What's her job?
B: She's a doctor. She's the doctor on *Icarus*.

A: Who are Yoko and Antonio? What are their jobs?
B: They're scientists. They're the scientists on *Icarus*.

D How old…?

Ask and answer questions about ages.

A: How old is Ivan Asimov?
B: He's forty (years old).
A: How old are Mark Ballard and Antonio Márquez?
B: They're thirty-two (years old).

E What's...nationality?

1. Complete the chart with these words:

Spanish French Japanese Russian
Brazilian British Chinese American

the United States	American
Russia	
Great Britain	
Spain	
China	
Japan	
Brazil	
France	

2. Ask and answer questions about nationalities and hometowns.

A: Mark Ballard is from Great Britain. What's his nationality?
B: He's British.
A: Where's he from in Great Britain?
B: He's from London.

F Thousands

6,000 six thousand
3,451 three thousand four hundred (and) fifty-one

Say these numbers:

2,987   2,000   3,820   4,361   8,510   10,000   1,207   9,001   5,100   9,400

G Interviews

Student A, you're a reporter. Student B, you're an *Icarus* crew member. Ask and answer questions about name, job, nationality, and hometown. Continue with other crew members.

H Game: Who is it?

Student A, make statements about crew members. Student B, guess who they are.

A: She's twenty-nine.
B: Is it Marie Verne?
A: No, it isn't. She's Brazilian.
B: Then it's Cristina Cabral.
A: That's right!

I Talk to your classmates.

Ask other students questions about their names, jobs, nationalities, and hometowns. Then write their answers.

SPACE TRAVEL—THE FACTS

1957
Laika, a dog, first traveler in space

1961
Yuri Gagarin, first man in space

1963
Valentina Tereshkova, first woman in space

1969
Neil Armstrong, first man on the moon

1973
Skylab space station

1975
Apollo-Soyuz, first joint U.S.-U.S.S.R. space project

1981
U.S. space shuttle, first orbital flight

E. What's...nationality?

1. Have students examine the chart and complete it by themselves.
2. Pair Work. Have students compare their answers.
3. Check answers by reviewing the chart with the class.
4. Have students read part 2.
5. Model the sample dialogue and have students repeat after you, chorally and individually.
6. Pair Work. Have students ask and answer questions about the crew members.
7. Check answers by reviewing the questions with the class.
8. In a multilingual class, ask: *What's my/your/his/her nationality?* In a monolingual class, use famous people.

   T: *Michael Jackson. What's his nationality?*
   S: *He's American.*

   Use currently famous living people: politicians, sports personalities, singers, entertainers, etc. Again, avoid asking: *What's Michael Jackson's nationality?* The possessive form is not taught until later in the book.

F. Thousands

1. Point out the example (*six thousand* not *six thousands*). Put the numbers on the board and get students to say them orally. Add more examples, if necessary.
2. Comprehension Dictation. Dictate these numbers. Have students write them down in numeric form.
   4,440 9,800 2,598 5,116 4,330 2,818 1,090 5,717 4,414

   Write the numbers on the board for students to self-correct.

G. Interviews

Role Play. Have students ask and answer questions, switching roles. Students can continue doing interviews as different crew members. Ask volunteers to demonstrate an interview in front of the class.

H. Game: Who is it?

1. Model the sample dialogue. Have students repeat after you, chorally and individually.
2. Pair Work. Have students alternate roles, guessing the identity of the crew member. Variation: Have individuals come to the front of the class and think of the name of one of the class members. The class has to guess the correct name. Streets or areas can be substituted for towns when all the students come from one town.

I. Talk to your classmates.

Pair Work. Have students interview each other and ask questions about their jobs, nationalities, and hometowns. Instruct students to write down the answers to the questions and report back to the class.

■ SPACE TRAVEL—THE FACTS

This material is designed for reading for pleasure. It is assumed that it will not be taught in class in any way. It is important for students to read information on occasions with no checking or testing. Of course, if student interest is aroused by the facts, you could spend time on them. Optional: With false beginners, use these facts to introduce the lesson.

■ WORKBOOK

The Workbook can be done for homework and checked in class. If you wish to use it in class, Exercises A, B, E, and G can be done as oral pair work.

What's it like?

Teaching points
Adjectives
What's it like?/What are they like?
It's big./They're big./It's a big car./They're big cars.
What color is it?
It's red./They're red.
It's a red car./They're red cars.
What kind is it?/are they?
It's a Corvette./They're Corvettes.
Nationalities (continued):
Colombian/Egyptian/Irish/Italian/Korean/Swedish/Swiss/Turkish
Ordinal numbers: *1st* to *8th*
Reading: The contest information contains incidental material to encourage students to read selectively.

Grammar note
Adjectives: In English, adjectives do not agree with the noun—*big car/big cars, new suitcase/new suitcases*. The choice of indefinite article depends on whether the word following it starts with a vowel sound, not on whether it is an adjective or a noun (see Unit 2):

an apple/a big apple
a drink/an orange drink

Expressions
good news
Fantastic!
What's it like?/What are they like?
Right.

Active vocabulary
beautiful/big/black/blue/brown/comfortable/contest/convertible/family car/fast/flag/gold/gray/green/jeans/letter (mail)/luxury/magazine/necklace/new/prize/red/shirt/silver/small/station wagon/sunglasses/sweater/van/weekend/what color/what kind/white/winner/worth/yellow

Passive vocabulary
describe/description/different/enter/giveaway/send/talk (about)/them/thing

Audiovisual aids
Cassette/CD
Realia: A number of colored objects

■ **ORAL INTRODUCTION**

Pre-teach the colors, using a collection of colored objects.

T: *It's a pen. It's red. It's a red pen.*, etc.

Ask: *What is it? What color is it?* about a number of objects.

■ **CONTEST FORM**

1. Have students examine the International Car Giveaway form. Get them to read the copy silently.

2. Ask the following questions: *What's the first prize? Where is it from? What's the second prize? Where is it from? What's the third prize? Where is it from? What's the fourth prize? Where is it from? What's the fifth prize? Where are they from? What's the sixth prize? Where is it from? What's the seventh prize? Where is it from? What's the name of the magazine? What's the address of the magazine?*

3. Have students complete the form and check the car that they would like to win. Also have them complete their name and address on the form. Check that they complete their address in the right sequence: name/street/city (town)/state or country/zip code.

■ **CONVERSATION (Kate, Paul)**

1. Have students examine the contest form again. Check that the text is covered.

2. Play the recording. Play it again, pausing for students to repeat, chorally and individually.

3. Demonstrate *What kind is it?* and *What color is it?* with realia, or classroom objects (the cassette player, a pen, a watch, a calculator, etc.). Ask questions: *What color's your (pen)? What kind is it? Ask him/her/me.*

continued

8 What's it like?

International Car Giveaway

7 Prizes

We're giving away 8 cars from 7 different countries

★ ★ ★

Enter Now!

seventh prize–Volkswagen Jetta, sedan, German, $13,400

first prize–Chevrolet Corvette ZR1, convertible, American $37,264

sixth prize–Toyota Previa, van, Japanese, $16,000

second prize–Jaguar XJ6, luxury car, British, $36,965

Are these your new cars?

fifth prize–two Hyundai Sonatas, family cars, Korean, $21,388

third prize–Volvo, station wagon, Swedish, $35,700

fourth prize–Peugeot, family car, French, $32,435

Write your name and address on the form and send it to: **International Car Giveaway**
Weekend Magazine
P.O. Box 54
St. Paul, MN 55101

Name: _____
Address: _____

Kate: Paul! Good news! I'm a winner in the contest!
Paul: What contest?
Kate: In *Weekend Magazine*.
Paul: What's your prize?
Kate: It's a new car!
Paul: A new car? What kind is it?
Kate: A Chevrolet Corvette!

Paul: Fantastic! What's it like?
Kate: It's a convertible. It's beautiful, it's fast, it's worth more than $37,000….
Paul: What color is it?
Kate: It's red.
Paul: And it's our car.
Kate: Well, *my* car.

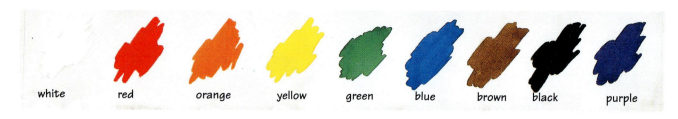

white | red | orange | yellow | green | blue | brown | black | purple

1st
a TV
brown
Samsung
Korean

2nd
jeans
blue
Levi's
American

3rd
a teacup
white
Wedgwood
British

4th
a watch
green
Swatch
Swiss

5th
sunglasses
black
Ray Ban
American

6th
a shirt
yellow
Lacoste
French

7th
a tie
gray
Giorgio Armani
Italian

8th
a camera
red
Konica
Japanese

A Role play

Look at the prizes.

- **A:** What's the (third)/(fifth) prize?
- **B:** It's a car/two cars.
- **A:** Fantastic! What kind is it/are they?
- **B:** It's (a Volvo)./They're (Hyundais).
- **A:** That's (Swedish), right?/Those are (Korean), right?
- **B:** Right.
- **A:** What's it like?/What are they like?
- **B:** It's a (station wagon)./They're (family cars).
- **A:** What color is it/are they?
- **B:** It's blue./They're white.

Talk about the other prizes.

B What kind is it?/What kind are they?

Ask and answer questions about the pictures.

- **A:** What's in the first picture?
- **B:** It's a TV.
- **A:** What color is it?
- **B:** It's brown.
- **A:** What kind is it?
- **B:** It's a Samsung.
- **A:** Is it Japanese?
- **B:** No, it isn't. It's Korean.

- **B:** What's in the second picture?
- **A:** They're jeans.
- **B:** What color are they?
- **A:** They're blue.
- **B:** What kind are they?
- **A:** They're Levi's.
- **B:** Are they British?
- **A:** No, they aren't. They're American.

4. Drill:

   T: *his watch*
   C: *What kind is it?*
   T: *the ties*
   C: *What kind are they?*
   Continue: *her watch/those pens/that cassette player/the stereo/that computer*

5. Drill:

   T: *the Corvette*
   C: *What color's the Corvette?*
   T: *the Sonatas*
   C: *What color are the Sonatas?*
   Continue: *Jaguar/Toyota/Volkswagen/Volvo*

6. Drill:

   T: *it*
   C: *What's it like?*
   T: *they*
   C: *What are they like?*
   Continue: *the car/the ties/the cassette player/the books*

7. Silent Reading.

8. Ask the following comprehension questions: *Is he the winner, or is she the winner? What's the prize? Is the car a Chevrolet? What kind is it? Is the car slow? Is it old? What's it like? Is it blue? Is it silver? Is it black? What color is it?*

9. Paired Reading. Make sure that students act out the conversation rather than read it.

■ COLORS

1. Review the colors at the top of the page. Point to various objects in the classroom and ask: *What color is it?*

2. Have students write the names of the colors on a piece of paper. Ask them to look around the class and categorize various objects by color. Give students 15 minutes to do this task. Make a master grid on the board and compare answers.

3. Expansion. Word Game. Write the colors in scrambled form. Get students to unscramble them (dre/*red*; ergen/*green*; lube/*blue*; weylol/*yellow*; clakb/*black*; lpruep/*purple*; theiw/*white*; worbn/*brown*). Time the game. The student who completes all scrambled words first is the winner.

A. Role play

1. Ask students to study the pictures of the prizes.

2. Explain ordinals to the class. Write *first, second, third, fourth, fifth, sixth, seventh, eighth, ninth,* and *tenth* on the board. Put the corresponding numerals next to the words. Talk about the relationship between the ordinals and the numbers.

3. Ask the following questions: *What is the first prize? Where's it from? What kind of car is it? How much is it? What's the second prize? Where's it from? What kind of car is it? How much is it?*, etc.

4. Pair Work. Have students role play conversations about the other prizes.

5. Expansion. Teach additional ordinals (*eleventh, twelfth, thirteenth,* etc.) and do dictation practice.

B. What kind is it?/What kind are they?

1. Write *1st, 2nd, 3rd,* etc. on the board. Point to each contracted form and have students say the full word.

2. Have students examine the first row of photographs. Check that the text below is covered. Ask the following questions: *What's in the first picture? What color is it? Is it a Panasonic? Is it a Sony? Is it French? Is it American? What nationality is it?*, etc. *What's in the second picture? What color are they? What kind are they?*, etc.

3. Have students uncover the text and read the conversations silently.

4. Pair Work. Have students ask and answer questions about pictures 1–4.

5. Pair Work. Have students continue asking and answering questions about pictures 5–8.

6. Expansion. Hold a discussion about ethnic food. Write various nationalities on the board: *Italian, Japanese, Mexican, Chinese, French, American, Vietnamese, German,* etc. Make sure that you use representative student countries. Ask students to tell you their favorite ethnic food. Tally all responses and make a final count: *Italian–15; Japanese–10;* etc.

Culture note: Talk about individual's reactions to foreign goods. Mention that many people do not like to purchase manufactured goods from other countries. They prefer to only buy items made and sold in their own country. This is especially true for thousands of Americans who will only purchase American made automobiles. On the other hand, many people enjoy buying foreign goods. They often feel that the items are better made and are a better value for their money.

C. Describe them.

1. Have students study the chart. Talk about the words that go together. Ask students if they see any other words on the chart that could describe some of these items: *big/small/jeans/shirt/sunglasses/shoes.* Also discuss why you don't use the word *comfortable* when describing TVs, suitcases, watches, and cameras.

2. Model the conversation. Have students repeat after you, chorally and individually.

3. Individualize the exercise and ask students about their own things. Encourage them to use the adjectives listed on the chart. Ask: *What's your pen like? What are your shoes like?*, etc.

4. Pair Work. Have students ask and answer questions about the items on the chart as well as their own things.

5. Write on the board: *It's big. It's a big car. They're big. They're big cars.* Get students to copy the sentences. Explain that the adjective does not agree with the noun. It always remains singular. Also explain that *a* and *an* relate to the next word, not to the noun: *an apple/a big apple; a car/an Italian car.*

6. Write on the board: *It's a car. It's Italian. It's an Italian car. It's an apple. It's big. It's a big apple.* Have students copy the sentences from the board. (For further practice, have students do the Workbook exercises as oral drills.)

7. Game. Ask each student to think of an object. Have the other students ask Yes/No questions until they can guess what the object is. *Is it red? Is it blue? Is it big? Is it expensive? Is it a car? Is it American? Is it a Corvette?*, etc. You can demonstrate the game with the whole class, and continue in pairs or small groups.

D. Flags

1. Do the exercise orally with the class.

2. Pair Work. Have students repeat the exercise, asking and answering questions.

   Culture note: The colors *red, white,* and *blue* are always referred to in that particular order when talking about the American and British flags. Mention that native speakers seldom change the order of these colors and think that it sounds odd to put them in a different order.

3. Expansion. Ask questions about other flags: *What color is your flag?* if it has not been included already.

■ WORKBOOK

The Workbook can be done for homework and checked in class. If you wish to use it in class, Exercises A, C, F, and G can be done as oral pair work.

C Describe them.

1. Study the words (big car, comfortable shirt) that can go together.
2. Describe your own things.

A: Our car's a Mazda. It's Japanese. It's small. It isn't new. It's not expensive.

B: My jeans are old. They're blue. They're Levi's. They're comfortable.

(not)	big	small	old	new	comfortable	expensive
car	✓	✓	✓	✓	✓	✓
TV	✓	✓	✓	✓		✓
suitcases	✓	✓	✓	✓		✓
jeans			✓	✓	✓	✓
shirt			✓	✓	✓	✓
watch	✓	✓	✓	✓		✓
camera	✓	✓	✓	✓		✓
sunglasses			✓	✓	✓	✓
shoes			✓	✓	✓	✓

D Flags

Ask and answer questions about the flags.

A: What color is the Turkish flag?
B: It's red and white.

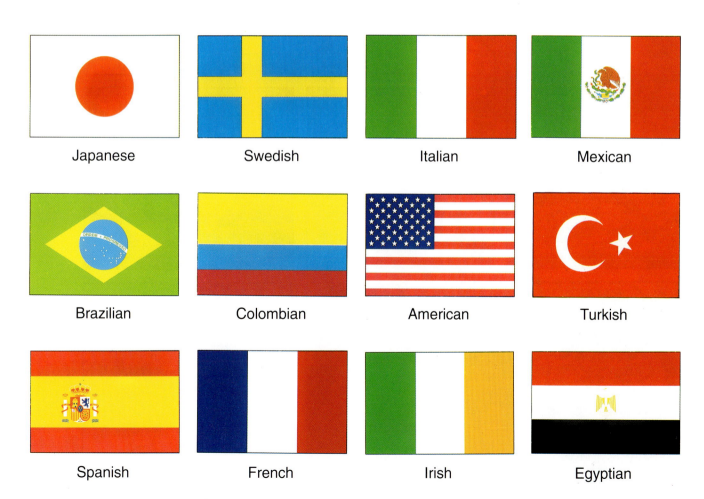

Japanese Swedish Italian Mexican

Brazilian Colombian American Turkish

Spanish French Irish Egyptian

9 Where is she?

Where is she?

> **Teaching points**
> Prepositions of place:
> *in/on/under/above/next to/in front of/behind/down/up*
> Object pronouns:
> *me/you/him/her/us/them/it*
> *Where is she?*
> *She's in front of me.*
> *Where are they?*
> *They're next to him.*
> *Who's behind us?*
> *They're behind us.*
> *Pull (them) up./Put (me) down.*
> Nationalities: *an/a/the American/Japanese/woman/runner now*
> Listening: task listening with limited aim, finding out the results of a race
> *In front* (adverbial) appears incidentally in the listening. Do not draw attention to it. It will be understood from *in front of.*
>
> **Grammar note**
> The main focus of this unit is object pronouns and prepositions.
> Nationality words ending in *-an* and *-ian* can function as adjectives or nouns: *American, an American runner.*
> Nationality words ending in *-ish, -ch,* and *-ese* only function as adjectives: *A British man. A man from Great Britain.*
>
> **Active vocabulary**
> *above/behind/copilot/crewman/dog/friendly/girl/ in front of/ocean/pull up/put down/rescue/rock/them/ under/us/water*
>
> **Passive vocabulary**
> *class/draw/helicopter/meter (measure)/race/seating chart/use (v.)*
>
> **Audiovisual aids**
> Cassette/CD
> Realia: boxes, colored pencils or pens

■ **CARTOON STRIP**

1. Have students examine the cartoon strip. Mention that it will not be possible to separate the text and the illustration as is usually done. Play the recording. Have students listen and follow the text and pictures. Play it again, pausing for students to repeat, chorally and individually.

2. Demonstrate the prepositions: *on/above, under, in, up/down.* Use a book, a table, and a bag. Ask: *Where is it now?* to elicit *It's on the table. Now it's above the table. It's under the bag. It's in the bag.,* etc. Repeat with two objects and ask: *Where are they now?* to elicit *They're on the table.,* etc.

3. Pair Work. Have students ask and answer questions, using a book, two pens, their table or desk, and a bag or briefcase.

4. Demonstrate object pronouns. Ask one male student and one female student to stand in the front of the class (or use board drawings). Indicate a male student and say: *Look at him.* Indicate a female student and say: *Look at her.* Point to yourself and say: *Look at me.* Move closer to the students (or move closer to the drawings on the board) and say: *Look at us.* Pick up an object and say: *Look at it.* Point as above and pause, looking confused. Elicit a choral response using the correct object pronoun. Demonstrate the phrases *put down* and *pull up.*

5. Have students examine the cartoon strip again. Play the recording, one frame or CD track at a time, pausing to ask questions.
   Note: On the CD, the is more than on frame per track.
   Frame 1
   T: *Is she in the ocean?*
   S1: *No, she isn't.*
   T: *Is she in the helicopter?*
   S2: *No, she isn't.*
   T: *Ask him, "Where?"*
   S3: *Where is she?*
   S4: *She's on the rock.*

continued

Unit 9   Teacher's Book ■ 28

Frame 2
T: *Is she above them or is she under them?*
Frame 3
T: *Is he above the helicopter or is he under the helicopter? Is she above him or is she under him?*
Frame 4
T: *Is she on the rock? Ask him, "Where?"*
Frame 5
T: *Is she on the water? Is she on the rock? Ask him, "Where?"*
Frame 6
T: *Are they in the helicopter? Are they in the ocean? Ask me, "Where?"*
Frame 7
T: *Ask him, "Where?"*
Frame 8
T: *Are they in the helicopter? Is the dog in the helicopter? Ask her, "Where?"*
Frame 9
T: *Where's the helicopter? Where's the man? What about the dog? Ask her, "Where?"*

6. Pair Work. Have students ask and answer questions about the cartoon strip.

7. Place an object in various spots in the classroom. Ask: *Where is it?* Repeat with two objects and ask: *Where are they?*

■ PREPOSITION DIAGRAMS

1. Copy the diagrams on the board. Make sure that students have closed their books. Ask students what the diagrams represent: *What's this?*

2. Have students open their books and study the diagrams silently.

3. Practice the prepositions by moving objects around a box on your desk. Continue asking questions about the placement of the objects until students are confident with the use of these prepositions.

4. Pair Work. Distribute boxes and objects to pairs for further practice.

5. Expansion. Send one student from the room. Hide an object, bring the student back into the classroom. Have the student ask questions: *Is it on the table? Is it next to the window? Is it front of (Maria)? Is it behind (Maria)? Is it in front of me? Is it behind me?* Have individuals or the class respond to the questions. Encourage the class to give hints to the student, such as *Hot* when the student is close or *Cold* when the student is not close. Variation: This game can be done in small groups.

A. Where are they?

1. Place four chairs in the front of the classroom. Put three chairs in a row, one behind the other. Put the fourth chair next to the middle one. Sit on the middle chair, have three volunteers sit in the other three chairs. Say:
I'm behind her. She's in front of me.
I'm in front of him. He's behind me.
I'm next to her. She's next to me.

2. Ask questions:

   T: *Where is she?*   C: *She's in front of you.*
   T: *Where is he?*   C: *He's behind you.*
   T: *Where am I?*   C: *You're behind her.*
   T: *and?*   C: *You're in front of him.*
   T: *and?*   C: *You're next to her.*

3. Have students examine the helicopter seating plan. Check vocabulary.

4. Model the conversation and have students repeat, chorally and individually.

5. Continue asking questions about the people in the plan.

6. Pair Work. Have students ask and answer questions about the plan.

7. Drill.

   T: *I'm here.*
   C: *Look at me.*
   T: *He's there.*
   C: *Look at him.*
   Continue: *She's here./We're here./They're over there./It's here.*

B. What's different?

1. Have students examine pictures A and B.

2. Read the example to the class. Point out the differences in the pictures.

3. Pair Work. Have students work together to find the differences in the two pictures. Circulate around the class to offer assistance, if necessary.

in on above under

next to up down behind in front of

A Where are they?

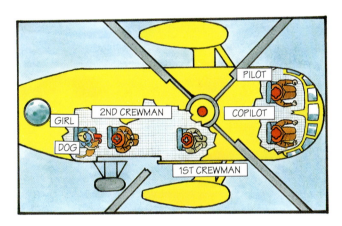

Ask and answer questions about the people in the helicopter. Use *Where* and *Who*.

A: Where's the second crewman?
B: He's behind the first crewman./He's in front of the girl./He's next to the door.
A: Who's behind the copilot?
B: The first crewman is behind the copilot.

B What's different?

Work with a partner. Look at picture A and picture B. What's different in picture B?

Student A: In picture A, the book on the TV is blue. In picture B, it's green.
Student B: In picture A, the cup is next to the newspaper. In picture B, it's on the newspaper.

29

C Draw a picture.

Draw ten things on the black and white picture. Work with another student. Ask and answer questions about your pictures.

A: Is there a book in your picture?
B: Yes, there is.
A: Is it on the TV?
B: No, it isn't.

D Your class

1. Look at this seating chart. Look at Maria.

   Who's behind her?
   Who's next to her?
   Who's in front of her?

   Ask and answer questions about the seating chart.

2. Now look at your class.

   Who's behind you?
   Who's next to you?
   Who's in front of you?

3. Draw a chart of your class. Ask and answer questions about your class.

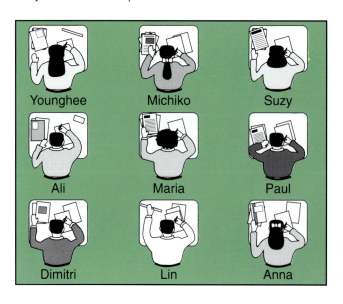

E Women's 200-meter race

Listen to the description of the race. Write the nationalities of the runners on the chart.

1st _____   4th _____

2nd _____   5th _____

3rd _____   6th _____

30

C. Draw a picture.

1. Have students examine the illustration.
2. Distribute colored pens or pencils so that students can use various colors on their pictures.
3. Pair Work. Have students work together to add details to the picture.
4. Model the conversation and have students repeat, chorally and individually.
5. Ask questions about students' drawings.

D. Your class

1. Have students examine the seating chart. Read the examples to the class.
2. Ask questions about the location of people on the chart.
3. Continue asking questions about the location of people in the classroom.

   T: *Where's (Fumiko)?*
   S1: *She's next to me./She's in front of you./She's behind (Pedro).*, etc.

4. Have students draw a seating plan and fill in the names of class members.
5. Pair Work. Have students ask and answer questions about the seating plan.
6. Writing. Encourage students to keep a list of prepositions in their notebooks. Have them draw diagrams like the one in this unit. When new prepositions are introduced, draw a diagram or visual on the board and have students copy it into their notebooks.

E. Women's 200-meter race

1. Have students examine the photograph.
2. In preparation for the listening activity, review the following nationalities: *Mexican, Japanese, British, Brazilian, American, Italian.* Note that when referring to nationalities ending with *-ian, -an,* and *-ese* you can say: *an Italian, an American, a Japanese.* However, with nationalities ending with *-ish* and *-ch* you must add another word: *the British woman.* Mention that students should feel free to use the additional word if they have any doubts about the correct form.
3. Explain the fact that students will be listening to a description of a race and that they must put the runners in the correct order. Note: the recording has a stopping point at the end of the race, then the results are announced. Play the tape/CD up to the stopping point twice. Give students time to note the order of the runners. Demonstrate and encourage the use of notes, like *M* for Mexican and *A* for American, etc. Finally, play the summary of the race on the tape/CD. Check answers by asking: *Who is first? Who is second?*, etc. If a student doesn't know, say: *Ask me/him/her.*

■ WORKBOOK

The Workbook can be done for homework and checked in class. Exercises A and G could be integrated into the lesson when looking at the preposition diagrams. If you wish to use the Workbook in class, Exercises A, B, and E can be done as oral pair work.

10 Quiz of the Week

> **Teaching points**
> There's (a camera) on the table./There are some (knives) on the table.
> There isn't (a telephone) on the table./There aren't any (telephones) on the table.
> Is there (an oven) on the table?
> Yes, there is./No, there isn't.
> Are there any (spoons or forks) on the table?
> Yes, there are./No, there aren't.
> What is the capital of (France)?
> Review of previously taught nouns and questions.
> Stand (next to me).
>
> **Expressions**
> Good evening.
> ladies and gentlemen
> Welcome to…
> Excuse me (to apologize)
> All right.
> Well,…
> Very good.
> That's terrific.
> Congratulations.
>
> **Active vocabulary**
> all/any/calculator/camera/capital/clock/contestant/else/fall (season)/just/last (adj.)/list (n.)/love/microwave/more/name (v.)/of/oil/open (v.)/or/oven/question (n.)/quiz/ready/second (time measurement)/singer/song/springtime/stand/table/telephone/there is/are/thing/think/think of/week/yours
>
> **Audiovisual aids**
> Cassette/CD
> Realia: paper bags and several objects

■ CONVERSATIONS 1 AND 2

1. Have students examine the illustrations. Check that the text is covered.

2. Play the recording for both conversations.

   Culture note: Game shows are popular on American daytime TV. Many of the game shows test contestants' knowledge of trivia. Some game shows are based on other areas of expertise: vocabulary, memory skills, consumer knowledge, etc. Oftentimes contestants win very big prizes (cars, boats, vacations) or large amounts of money. Contestants who appear on TV are generally chosen for both their knowledge and their "on screen" enthusiasm.

■ CONVERSATION 1

1. Play the tape/CD for the first part of the conversation again. Make sure that students cover the text.

2. Silent Reading.

3. Ask the following questions: *What's his name? Are there any prizes? What are they like? Who is the first contestant? What's his first name? What's his last name? Is he from New York? Ask him/her, "where?" Is he behind him? Ask him/her, "where?"*

4. Write on the board:
   Question 1:   right   wrong
   Question 2:   right   wrong
   Question 3:   right   wrong

   Have students circle the answers.

5. Ask the following questions: *What's the first question? Ask him/her. What's the answer? Is that right? What's the second question? Ask him/her. What's the answer? Is that right? What's the third question? Ask him/her. What's the answer? Is that right?*

6. Paired Reading.

■ CONVERSATION 2

1. Have students examine the illustration. Play the second part of the conversation again.

2. Make the following *true/false* statements and have students respond *right* or *wrong* (or *true* or *false*). *There's a picture. There are some knives. There's a microwave oven. There are some forks. There aren't any spoons. There isn't a calculator. There's a telephone.*

continued

10 Quiz of the Week

1.
Alex: Good evening, ladies and gentlemen. I'm Alex Beck. Welcome to *Quiz of the Week!* Our first contestant is Andy Miller, from Springfield. Hello, Andy. How are you?
Andy: I'm fine, thanks, Alex.
Alex: Excuse me, Andy. You're in front of me. Stand next to me, please.
Andy: Sorry.
Alex: OK, here's your first question. What's the capital of France?
Andy: Uh…uh…I don't know.
Alex: Think of the song, Andy. "I love *Paris* in the springtime, I love *Paris* in the fall."
Andy: Is it Paris?
Alex: Yes, that's right, Andy! And now your second question. Where's Brasilia?
Andy: Uh, I think it's in Brazil.
Alex: Right! And now your third and last question. Who's Michael Jackson?
Andy: He's a singer.
Alex: That's right! Open the doors!

2.
Alex: OK, Andy. Look at the things on the table for ten seconds. Then name all of them in thirty seconds, and they're yours. Ready?
Alex: All right, Andy. What is there on the table?
Andy: Well, there's a picture. It's an oil painting. And there's a camera. And there's a clock. A gold clock.
Alex: Very good. What else is there?
Andy: Uh…uh…
Alex: Is there an oven?
Andy: Yes, there is! There's a microwave oven! And uh…. Are there any spoons or forks on the table?
Alex: No, there aren't any spoons or forks, but…. Come on, Andy!
Andy: There are some knives!
Alex: That's terrific, Andy. OK, there's just one more thing on the table.
Andy: There's a…. Is there a telephone? No, there isn't a telephone. I know! There's a calculator!
Alex: Congratulations, Andy! Come and look at your prizes!

A Game: What is there in the picture?

1. Student A, look at picture one for thirty seconds. Close your book. Student B, ask Student A, "What is there in the first picture?"

2. Student B, look at picture two for thirty seconds. Close your book. Student A, ask Student B, "What is there in the second picture?"

B Is there…?/Are there…?

Ask and answer questions about pictures one and two.

A: Is there a gold clock in picture one?
B: Yes, there is.
A: Is there a camera in picture two?
B: No, there isn't.
A: Are there any watches in picture two?
B: No, there aren't.
A: Are there any knives in picture one?
B: Yes, there are.

C Write a list.

Look at the three pictures. Write a list of ten things in them.

1. _____   6. _____
2. _____   7. _____
3. _____   8. _____
4. _____   9. _____
5. _____   10. _____

Talk to another student. Ask and answer questions about your lists.

Is there a/an _____ on your list?
Yes, there's a/an _____ on my list.
No, there isn't a/an _____ on my list.

Are there any _____ on your list?
Yes, there are some _____.
No, there aren't any _____.

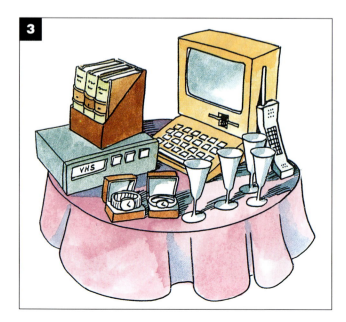

3. Silent Reading.

4. Have students look at the top illustration on the next page. Ask the following questions to elicit: *Yes, there is./No, there isn't./Yes, there are./No, there aren't.*
   Is there a microwave oven? Is there a computer? Is there a table? Is there a telephone? Is there a CD player? Is there a clock? Is there a pen? Is there a book? Is there a calculator? Are there any pictures? Are they any spoons? Are they any clocks? Are they any suitcases? Are there any cassette players? Are there any knives? Are there any TVs?

5. Pair Work. Have students ask and answer questions as above.

6. Paired Reading.

7. Pair Work. Have one student in each pair close their book, and role play the part of the contestant. Have the other student role play the part of the quiz show host, using the illustration at the top of the next page as reference.

A. Game: What is there in the picture?

1. Explain that the students will be using the illustrations for a game similar to the quiz show on the previous page.

2. Pair Work. Have Student A study picture one for 30 seconds and then close the book. Have Student B ask Student A to name all of the objects in the picture.

3. Pair Work. Have Student B study picture two for 30 seconds and close the book. Have Student A ask Student B to name all of the objects in the picture.

4. Have the entire class study picture three for 30 seconds and close their books. Ask volunteers to name all of the objects in the picture.

B. Is there…?/Are there…?

1. Model the conversations for the class.

2. Pair Work. Have students ask and answer questions about pictures one and two.

3. Check comprehension by asking students several questions about each picture.

C. Write a list.

1. Explain the directions to the class.

2. Have students work individually to compose a list of ten items from pictures one, two, and three.

3. Pair Work. Have students ask and answer questions based on their lists. Encourage them to model their questions and responses on the examples in the book.

4. Language Summary. Write the following sentences on the board: *There's a pen on the table. There are some books on the table. There isn't a bag on the table. There aren't any cups on the table. Is there a pen on the table? Yes, there is./No, there isn't. Are there any books on the table? Yes, there are./No, there aren't.* Have students copy the sentences in their notebooks.

5. Expansion. Game: What's in the bag? Place five singular objects (book, watch, apple, orange, fork) and five pairs of objects (pens, knives, spoons, cassettes, pencils) into a paper bag.

   Variation A: Have students ask questions until they discover what is in the bag.

   Variation B: Show students the contents of the bag. Have them make statements until they name all of the objects.

   Variation C: Have students play this game in small groups. Distribute a variety of bags to groups and have them fill the bag with objects. Encourage groups to come to the front of the class and play the game with the rest of the class.

   S1: *Are there any pens in the bag?*
   S2: *Yes, there are.*
   T: *What are they like?/What color are they?*
   S1: *There's a blue pen, and there are two gold pens.*
   T: *Is that right?*
   S2: *No, it isn't. There are two blue pens, and a red pen.*

D. A quiz

1. Explain the directions and model the conversations for the class.

2. Pair Work. Have students work together to ask and answer questions. Encourage students to answer with complete sentences.

E. Write a quiz.

1. Silent Reading.

2. Have students write six new questions. Offer assistance, if necessary.

3. Pair Work. Have students work together to ask and answer their questions.

   Variation: Divide the class into an even number of groups. Have each group compose six questions based on the models. Conduct a competitive group quiz.

■ WORKBOOK

The Workbook can be done for homework and checked in class. If you wish to use it in class, Exercises A and C can be done as oral pair work.

D A quiz

Student A, cover Student B's questions. Student B, cover Student A's questions. Take turns asking and answering your questions.

A: What's the capital of France?
B: It's Paris.
A: That's right.
B: What color is the Swedish flag?
A: (I think) It's blue and white. (I don't know.)
B: (No, it isn't.) It's blue and yellow.

STUDENT A

1. What's the capital of the United States?
   It's Washington, D.C.
2. What nationality is Steven Spielberg?
   He's American.
3. Where's Bangkok?
   It's in Thailand.
4. Who's Janet Jackson?
   She's a singer.
5. What color is the Italian flag?
   It's green, white, and red.

STUDENT B

1. Where's Princess Diana from?
   She's from Great Britain.
2. What color is the Japanese flag?
   It's red and white.
3. Who's Placido Domingo?
   He's a singer.
4. What's the capital of Mexico?
   It's Mexico City.
5. What nationality is Yoko Ono?
   She's Japanese.

E Write a quiz.

Write six new questions. Work with a new partner. Take turns asking your quiz questions.

1. What's the capital of _____?
   It's _____.
2. What nationality is _____?
   He's/She's _____.
3. Where's _____?
   It's in _____.
4. Where's _____ from?
   He's/She's from _____.
5. What color is the _____ flag?
   It's _____.
6. Who's _____?
   He's/She's a _____.

Checkback — Units 1–10

A Which verb?

Fill in the blanks with the correct verbs.

1. He _____ from France.
   a. 'm   b. 's   c. 're
2. _____ you from Canada?
   a. Am   b. Is   c. Are
3. Where _____ they from?
   a. am   b. is   c. are
4. I _____ fine, thanks.
   a. 'm   b. 's   c. 're
5. It _____ a camera.
   a. 'm   b. 's   c. 're
6. _____ she a teacher?
   a. Am   b. Is   c. Are
7. We _____ police officers.
   a. 'm   b. 's   c. 're
8. Yes, I _____.
   a. am   b. is   c. are
9. _____ that a helicopter?
   a. Am   b. Is   c. Are
10. Yes, they _____.
    a. am   b. is   c. are

B Negative sentences

It's a hamburger. *It isn't a hamburger.*

Make these sentences negative.

1. I'm from the United States.
2. These are apples.
3. We're late.
4. That's a calculator.
5. It's a star.
6. He's a teacher.
7. Those are our suitcases.
8. You're right.
9. This is my car.
10. She's from Japan.

C Numbers

Complete the chart.

	cardinals	ordinals
1.	one	_____
2.	two	_____
3.	_____	third
4.	_____	fourth
5.	five	_____
6.	six	_____
7.	_____	seventh
8.	eight	_____
9.	_____	ninth

D What time is it?

1. *It's ten-fifty.*

2. _____   3. _____

4. _____   5. _____

Checkback Units 1–10

■ **ANSWER KEY**

This answer key may be photocopied.
No other part of this publication may be photocopied without the prior written consent of Oxford University Press.
Please do not write on this answer key.

A. Which verb?

1. 's
2. Are
3. are
4. 'm
5. 's
6. Is
7. 're
8. am
9. Is
10. are

B. Negative sentences

1. I'm not from the United States.
2. These aren't apples.
3. We aren't late.
4. That isn't a calculator.
5. It isn't a star.
6. He isn't a teacher.
7. These aren't our suitcases.
8. You aren't right.
9. This isn't my car.
10. She isn't from Japan.

C. Numbers

	cardinals	ordinals
1.	one	first
2.	two	second
3.	three	third
4.	four	fourth
5.	five	fifth
6.	six	sixth
7.	seven	seventh
8.	eight	eighth
9.	nine	ninth

D. What time is it?

1. It's ten-fifty.
2. It's two-fifteen.
3. It's seven thirty-five.
4. It's twelve-twenty.
5. It's eight twenty-five.

E. Question words

1. How much
2. Who
3. How
4. Where
5. What kind
6. When
7. What

F. Plural sentences

1. They're one-way tickets.
2. They're red cars.
3. They're tuna sandwiches.
4. They're eggs.
5. They're big rooms.

G. A, an, any

1. Are there any cassettes in the pictures?
   There's a cassette in the second picture.
   There aren't any cassettes in the first picture.
2. Are there any apples in the pictures?
   There's an apple in the first picture.
   There aren't any apples in the second picture.
3. Are there any oranges in the pictures?
   There's an orange in the first picture.
   There aren't any oranges in the second picture.
4. Are there any calculators in the pictures?
   There's a calculator in the second picture.
   There aren't any calculators in the first picture.
5. Are there any sandwiches in the pictures?
   There's a sandwich in the first picture.
   There aren't any sandwiches in the second picture.

E Question words

Fill in the blanks with these question words.

How   When
How much   Where
What   Who
What kind

1. _____ is the pizza?
   75¢ a slice.
2. _____'s that?
   My English teacher.
3. _____ do you spell your last name?
4. _____'s she from?
5. I have a new computer.
   _____ is it?
   A Macintosh.
6. _____'s the next train for Omaha?
   At 7:07.
7. _____'s his phone number?
   555-5280.

F Plural sentences

It's a taxi.   *They're taxis.*

Make these sentences plural.

1. It's a one-way ticket.
2. It's a red car.
3. It's a tuna sandwich.
4. It's an egg.
5. It's a big room.

G A, an, any

(telephone)
Are there any telephones in the pictures?
There's a telephone in the second picture.
There aren't any telephones in the first picture.

Look at the pictures. Write questions and answers. Use the cues in parentheses ( ). Score one point for each correct question and one point for each correct answer.

1. (cassette)
2. (apple)
3. (orange)
4. (calculator)
5. (sandwich)

35

H Pronouns and possessives

Complete the chart.

I	____	my
____	you	____
we	____	____
____	him	his
she	____	____
____	them	____

I Talking about grammar

Circle the correct letter, *a* or *b*. You can look at the grammar summaries for Units 1–10 for help. Score *two* points for each correct answer.

1. Am I early?
   Am is
   a. a singular verb.
   b. a plural verb.

2. He's an engineer.
   An is
   a. a definite article.
   b. an indefinite article.

3. There aren't any knives on the table.
   Knives is
   a. a regular plural.
   b. an irregular plural.

4. His jeans are blue.
   His is
   a. a personal pronoun.
   b. a possessive adjective.

5. They're in Los Angeles.
   They is
   a. the subject.
   b. the object.

J Locations

(Mr. Wong, Mrs. Wong)
Mr. Wong is next to Mrs. Wong.

Write sentences. Use the cues in parentheses ( ).
Use *next to*, *behind*, and *in front of*.

1. (Mr. Wong, Kevin)
2. (Mrs. Wong, Mr. Wong)
3. (Melissa, Mrs. Wong)
4. (Mrs. Wong, Melissa)
5. (Kevin, Mr. Wong)

H. Pronouns and possessives

I	*me*	*my*
you	you	*your*
we	*us*	our
he	him	his
she	*her*	her
they	them	*their*

I. Talking about grammar

1. a singular verb.
2. an indefinite article.
3. an irregular plural.
4. a possessive adjective.
5. the subject.

J. Locations

1. Mr. Wong is behind Kevin.
2. Mrs. Wong is next to Mr. Wong.
3. Melissa is in front of Mrs. Wong.
4. Mrs. Wong is behind Melissa.
5. Kevin is in front of Mr. Wong.

K. Expressions 1

1. No, thank you.
2. Hello.
3. Thanks.
4. You're welcome.
5. A fruit salad, please.
6. Good night.
7. fine, thanks.
8. That's OK.

L. Expressions 2

1. Stacey (Unit 5)
2. Diana (Unit 6)
3. clerks (Unit 2)
4. Paul (Unit 8)
5. Alex Beck (Unit 10)
6. woman (Unit 6)

K Expressions 1

Choose the best response from the box below.

1. Coffee?
   _____

2. Hello.
   _____

3. Here you are.
   _____

4. Thank you.
   _____

5. Can I help you?
   _____

6. Good night.
   _____

7. How are you?
   _____

8. Sorry.
   _____

A fruit salad, please.	No, thank you.
Fine, thanks.	Thanks.
Good night.	That's OK.
Hello.	You're welcome.

L Expressions 2

Look at these expressions from Units 1–10.
Who uses them? Match.

Expression
1. Well, we're *on time*.
2. *Excuse me, are these seats taken?*
3. *Anything else?*
4. *Fantastic!*
5. *Come on,* Andy!
6. That's it *over there*.

Speaker
a. clerks (Unit 2)
b. woman (Unit 6)
c. Diana (Unit 6)
d. Alex Beck (Unit 10)
e. Stacey (Unit 5)
f. Paul (Unit 8)

SCORE (out of 100) _____ %

11 Is there any...?

In English, some things are *countable*, and some things are *uncountable*.

Countable

1   There's an orange in the picture.
2, 3, 4...   There are some tomatoes in the picture.
          There are three tomatoes.

tomatoes 3   orange 1   apple 0

Uncountable

There's some milk in the picture.
There isn't any coffee.

milk ✓   coffee ✗

A Chart

Look at the picture, and complete this chart.

potatoes	4	sandwich	____	butter	____	peas	____
cheese	✓	bread	____	lemon	____	soda	____
tea	____	eggs	____	meat	____	apple juice	____
chicken	____	water	____	tuna	____	cookies	____

11 Is there any...?

Teaching points
Countable/uncountable nouns:
There's an orange./There isn't an orange.
There aren't any oranges.
There's some milk./There isn't any milk.
Is there a lemon?/Are there any lemons?/Is there any milk?
in the bowl/the pitcher/the refrigerator/San Miguel
on the plate
Review of food vocabulary.
Listening: Pre-task to focus attention, then for specific information.
Reading: From notes, expanding notes orally into full sentences.

Grammar note
This lesson starts with an explanation of countable/uncountable nouns in order to focus the students on this point of grammar. Students have an opportunity to explore this information themselves in the *Perfect pizza* section.

Expressions
be on the phone (with someone)

Active vocabulary
airport/anchovies/antibiotics/bad/banana/bandage/bowl (n.)/bread/breakfast/broccoli/butter/clean (adj.)/clothing/corn flakes/dinner/dough/electricity/equipment/food/gas/helicopter/hospital/juice/lemon/lettuce/lunch/meat/medicine/mushroom/nurse/olive/onion/pea/perfect/pickle/pineapple/pizza/potato/sausage/shrimp/tea/tomato/tomato sauce/volcano

Passive vocabulary
call/chooose/countable/deliver/design (v.)/exercise/false/give/large/medium/news report/notebook/order/sentence/uncountable

Audiovisual aids
Cassette/CD
Realia: pitcher of water and two cups for Oral introduction.

■ ORAL INTRODUCTION

Take in a pitcher of water and two cups. Point to them and say: *There's a pitcher. There are two cups. There's some water in the pitcher. There isn't any water in the cups.*

Pour all of the water into the two cups. Continue: *Is there any water in the pitcher? No, there isn't. Is there any water in the cups? Yes, there is.*

Model the key sentences again, pausing for students to repeat chorally.

■ INTRODUCTION: COUNTABLE AND UNCOUNTABLE

Focus attention on the picture. Go through the explanation of countable and uncountable nouns. Write *How many?* and *How much?* on the board. Ask: *How many oranges are there? There are three. How much milk is there? There is some.* Model again, pausing for students to repeat.

A. Chart

1. Direct students' attention to the chart. Go over the examples (potatoes/cheese) to check that they know what to do. Have students work individually to complete the chart.

2. Ask students to exchange books to check their answers or check the answers yourself.

B. Is there a lemon in the picture?

1. Ask students about what is in the picture to elicit: *Yes, there is./No, there isn't./Yes, there are./No, there aren't.*

2. Drill:

   T: *milk*
   C: *There's some milk.*
   T: *potatoes*
   C: *There are some potatoes.*
   Continue: *eggs/water/cheese/cookies*

3. Pair Work. Have students ask and answer questions about the picture in pairs, changing roles.

4. Ask pairs to ask and answer questions in front of the class.

C. True or false?

1. Ask students to look carefully at the picture of breakfast. Direct their attention to the *true/false* exercise. Give students time to complete the exercise individually.
   Note: This is the first time students have seen the negative sentence in full.

2. Check the answers by quickly saying each statement in the book and eliciting *true* or *false* from the class.

3. Explain the pair work section. Student A is to write a similar true-false exercise about lunch, Student B about dinner, then get his/her partner to complete it. Model an example to make sure students know what to do.

4. Pair Work. Students complete the exercise in pairs.

5. Check the statements and answers by calling on pairs to read in front of the class.

6. Drill (optional):

   T: *coffee*
   C: *There isn't any coffee.*
   T: *eggs*
   C: *There aren't any eggs.*
   Continue: *sugar/orange juice/corn flakes*

D. Breakfast, lunch, and dinner

1. Ask students to ask and answer questions about the pictures in pairs, as in B above. Model asking and answering the questions in the book first.

2. Expansion. Ask students to write lists of what they eat each day. On the board write *My Breakfast, My Lunch, My Dinner.*

3. Pair Work. Have students ask and answer questions about each other's lists using the structures *Is there any (milk) on your list?/Are there any (eggs) on your list?*
   Note: At this stage students don't know the structures to ask *Do you have milk for breakfast?* Asking about the lists gives additional practice of the structures they do know.

E. What's in the refrigerator?

1. Explain the activity carefully.

2. Draw students' attention to the picture of the refrigerator. Ask students to speculate what might be in the refrigerator. Give students time to list five countable and five uncountable things.
   Note: Point out there are no right or wrong answers here. They are only to write down what might be there.

3. Tell students to listen carefully to the conversation and check off the things on their list that are in the refrigerator. Explain they should not check off something that is mentioned, but is not in the refrigerator.
   Note: Emphasize it is irrelevant how many items they can check off; i.e., their list might be completely different from what is actually in the refrigerator. The purpose here is to focus students on the vocabulary and to give them practice listening attentively for specific information.

4. Play the recording once. Students check off the items. Say: *There is some butter./There are some tomatoes./There is some fruit./There are some eggs./There is some cheese./There is some milk.*

5. Play the recording again, pausing for students to confirm what *is* in the refrigerator according to the tape.

6. Ask volunteers what items on their lists were in the refrigerator.
   Note: Emphasize this is only for fun; it is not a quiz!

7. Expansion. Game: In groups have students prepare a tray (or a paper or plastic bag) with some countable things and some uncountable things on (in) it. Have each group show the tray to another group for 30 seconds. Students then have to recall contents of the tray. They can ask questions: *Is there any…?/Are there any…?/Are there some…?* Students can change the contents and repeat with other groups.

B Is there a lemon in the picture?

Ask and answer questions about the picture on page 38.

A: Is there a lemon in the picture?
B: Yes, there is./No, there isn't.
A: Are there any bananas?
B: No, there aren't./Yes, there are.
A: Is there any lettuce?
B: Yes, there is./No, there isn't.

C True or false?

1. Look at the picture of breakfast. Are these sentences true (T) or false (F)?

    1. There are two eggs on the plate.
    2. There's some coffee in the cup.
    3. There are some corn flakes in the bowl.
    4. There isn't any bread on the plate.
    5. There isn't any milk in the bowl.
    6. There's some butter on the plate.

2. Student A, write a true-false exercise about lunch. Give it to Student B. Student B, write a true-false exercise about dinner. Give it to Student A. Check your answers.

D Breakfast, lunch, and dinner

Look at Exercise B. Ask and answer questions about breakfast, lunch, and dinner.

Are there any corn flakes for breakfast?
Is there a sandwich for dinner?
Is there any soda for lunch?

E What's in the refrigerator?

1. Guess what's in the refrigerator. Write a list with five countable things and five uncountable things.

2. Now listen to the conversation about the refrigerator. Check (✓) the things that are in the refrigerator and on your list.

F   The perfect pizza?

1. Look at the picture. What things are countable? What things are uncountable? Make sentences about the picture.

   There's some pizza dough in the picture.
   There are some olives.

2. What's the perfect pizza for you? Think of your answer. Then ask another student.

   A: What's on your perfect pizza?
   B: Well, there's tomato sauce on it, and there's cheese. There are some onions. There aren't any anchovies….

G   News report

Listen to this news report.

Good evening. This is Amy Walker for the six o'clock news. I'm in San Miguel. That's the volcano behind me. It's very bad here. There isn't any gas or electricity, and there isn't any clean water. There are five hundred people in the hospital, and there isn't any medicine there. There are some helicopters from the U.S. at the airport. There's some food and there are some antibiotics on the helicopters. Our next report from San Miguel will be at nine o'clock.

Look at Ms. Walker's notes. You're in the U.S. You're on the phone with her. Ask her about San Miguel. Ask her about the helicopters.

TV report—six o'clock

IN SAN MIGUEL—NOT ANY
gas/electricity/clean water/medicine/nurses/rescue
equipment

ON THE HELICOPTERS—SOME
food/antibiotics/clothing/bandages/doctors/nurses

F. The perfect pizza?

1. Focus attention on the picture of the pizza. Ask students to decide which things are countable and which are uncountable. In pairs have students make sentences about the pizza with: *There's some…/ There are some….*

   Note: Explain the difference between *a green pepper* versus *some green peppers* versus *some green pepper* by drawing on the board one pepper, three peppers, and some very small bits of diced pepper. *Some pepper* is used here to indicate that it is part of a whole, not that it is uncountable in the same sense as *water*.

2. Have students study *The Perfect Pizza* order form and design their own pizzas individually. Make sure they are clear about the meaning of *You choose!* by asking students what the choices are.

3. Pair Work. Have students ask each other about their choice of pizza.

4. Role Play. Have pairs of students role play the conversation between the clerk at the pizza shop and a customer. Demonstrate:

   A: *Yes?*
   B: *A pizza please.*
   A: *What with?*
   B: *Mushrooms and shrimp, please.*
   A: *What's your name? Your address? Your phone number?*

   Encourage students to use gestures and realia (a pad of paper and a pencil, etc.).

5. Ask pairs to demonstrate for the class.

G. News report

1. Direct students' attention to the picture. Check that the text is covered.

2. Have students speculate about what is happening. Ask: *Where is she? Who is she? What is going on?*

3. Write on the board for students to copy: *gas, electricity, airplanes, medicine, helicopters, doctors, water*. Tell students they are going to listen to a news report. They should put a check next to any of these words that are in the report.

4. Play the report. Have students complete the task.

5. Silent Reading.

6. Have students check their answers to the pre-listening activity.

7. Play the report again as a final check.

8. Ask individually or of the class: *What time is it? What is her name? Where is she? What is it like in San Miguel? Is there any gas? Is there any clean water? Is there any medicine in the hospital? Is there any food? Are there any helicopters? Where are the helicopters? When is the next report?*

9. Silent reading of Ms. Walker's notebook. Check the vocabulary.

10. Role Play. In pairs, students role play a conversation between Ms. Walker and the TV station in the U.S.

11. Dictate: *There are some doctors. They're from the U.S. There are some nurses. They're American. There are 500 people in the hospital. They're hurt. There isn't any medicine. There are antibiotics on the helicopters.*

12. Check answers on the board. Make sure students spell *they're* and *their* correctly.

■ WORKBOOK

The Workbook can be done for homework and checked in class. If you wish to use it in class, Exercises E and G can be done as oral pair work.

12 The Family

Teaching points
I/you/we/they/have a sister/some sisters.
He/she doesn't have a sister/any sisters.
I/you/we/they/don't have a sister/any sisters.
Do you/they have a sister/any sisters?
Does he/she have a sister/any sisters?
Short answers:
Yes, I/we/you/they do.
No, I/we/you/they don't.
Yes, he/she does.
No, he/she doesn't.
Review of possessive adjectives, plus genitive ('s).
It's John's car. It's his car. They're John's children. They're John and Mary's children.
It's Charles's house. They're Charles's children.
What's (your) favorite color?
Who's (your) favorite singer? Who are your favorite singers?
Family and Relations: see vocabulary below.
Reading: simple texts.

Grammar note
The main focus here is *has/doesn't have*, which is standard spoken American English. Words ending with sibilants (*s* and *z*) can add an apostrophe (') without an *s*; e.g., *James' car, Carlos' book*. The generally accepted form is *Charles's*, which is taught here, although *Charles'* is used as well.

Expressions
be married to

Active vocabulary
apartment/athlete/aunt/brother/businessman/cat/child/ country/cousin/daughter/factory/father/favorite/friend/ good/grandchild/grandfather/grandmother/grandparents/ happy/house/husband/model/money/mother/near/nephew/ nice/niece/parent/person/pet/program/ranch/rich/rock singer/sister/son/sport/uncle/very/wife/writer

Passive vocabulary
episode/fabulous/family/postcard/series/studio/watch (v.)

Audiovisual aids
This unit is not recorded.
Realia: a bag, books, and pens for introduction

■ ORAL INTRODUCTION

Note: This section should be done at a lively pace as a warm-up exercise.
Optional: With false beginners, steps 2–5 can be skipped.

1. Take a few small items into class. Put them on a table. Say: *I have a bag, I have a book,* and *I have some pens. How about you?*
   Indicate various students to elicit sentences with: *I have....*
   Indicate a student, say: *You have a bag. You have some books. How about me?*
   Go to a student, say: *He has a pen. He has some books.*
   And (Jiro)?
   Indicate a male student to elicit sentences with: *He has....*
   Repeat with a female student: *She has....*
   Indicate two students, say: *They have some pens. They have some books. How about (George) and (Maria)?*
   Indicate various students to elicit: *They have....*
   Stand next to a student, say: *We have some pens, we have some books. How about you?*
   Indicate pairs of students to elicit: *We have....*

2. Drill:
   T: *I*
   C: *I have some pens.*
   Continue: *she/we/they/he/you/I/(Maria)*

3. Say: *I don't have a cassette player. I don't have any cassettes.*
   Indicate a student. *She (he) doesn't have a cassette player. She (he) doesn't have any cassettes.*
   Continue, using singular and plural negative examples: *I don't have a (pen). They don't have any (pens).*

4. Drill:
   T: *He*
   C: *He doesn't have any cassettes.*
   Continue: *they/I/she/we/Jiro/you*

continued

12 The Family

TV NEWS
October 16th
CBC's new television series,
The Family
Wednesdays, 8:00–8:30 PM

George is a very rich man. He has a computer factory near New York. He's married to Janet. They have three children, two sons and a daughter. Janet and George have an apartment in New York, and he has a ranch in Texas.

George Howe

Janet Howe

Janet is George's wife. She's a writer of mystery novels, and she's very rich, too. She has a house in the country, and she has two cars, a convertible and a station wagon.

Charles and Linda Howe

Patricia and James Williams

Robert Howe
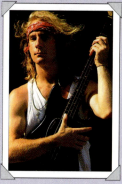

Charles is their son. He's 36. His wife's name is Linda. They have two children. Linda's a famous model. Charles is a good businessman, but he isn't a nice person. He doesn't have any friends.

Patricia is George and Janet's daughter. She's her father's favorite child. She's a scientist. Patricia's 32. James is Patricia's husband. He's a doctor.

Robert is Charles and Patricia's brother. He's a rock singer, but he isn't famous. His father isn't happy about Robert's job. Robert doesn't have any children, and he doesn't have any money. He's 25. He's his mother's favorite child.

Lisa and David

Peter and Ashley

They're Charles's children. Patricia is their aunt. Robert is their uncle. David is Patricia's nephew, and Lisa's her niece. Lisa is seven, and her brother is six. They have two pets—a dog and a cat.

They're Lisa and David's cousins. They're Patricia's children. Peter's four, and his sister is two. George is their grandfather, and Janet is their grandmother. They don't have any pets.

The Family
Contest

Win our fabulous first prize! Dinner with the actors in **The Family** at the CBC Studio!!

Are these sentences true (T) or false (F)?

1. George is Robert's father.
2. Peter is Charles's son.
3. David is Robert's nephew.
4. Charles is Ashley's uncle.
5. Lisa is Patricia's niece.
6. Patricia is Janet's daughter.
7. Robert is Janet's grandson.
8. Lisa is George's granddaughter.
9. Patricia and James are Peter's parents.
10. Janet and George are Charles's grandparents.
11. Linda is Charles's wife.
12. James is Linda's husband.

Answer these questions about The Family.

13. Who's Janet's daughter?
14. Who are Janet's sons?
15. Who's James's wife?
16. Who's Linda's husband?
17. Who's Lisa's brother?
18. Who's Charles and Robert's sister?
19. Who are Charles's parents?
20. Who's Charles's niece?
21. Who are Robert's nephews?
22. Who are Peter's cousins?

Write your answers on a postcard, and send them to TV NEWS.
Watch the first episode of **The Family** for the address.

A Contest

1. Write your answers to the contest questions.
2. Check your answers with another student.

A: Is George Robert's father?
B: Yes, he is. Number 1 is true.
A: Who's Janet's daughter?
B: Patricia.

B Family

Ask and answer more questions, with these words:

grandfather	son
grandmother	daughter
grandparents	grandson
parents	granddaughter
children	grandchildren
father	niece
mother	nephew
brother	uncle
sister	aunt
husband	cousin
wife	

42

5. Say: *Do you have a watch?* Repeat. *Does she have a watch?* Ask me. (Point to your watch) to elicit from the class: *Do you have a watch?* Say: *Yes, I do.* Ask questions: *Do you have a watch/radio/any pens/any books/a car/a dog?*, to elicit: *Yes I do/No, I don't.*
Ask the above questions of the class and of individuals.

■ TEXTS: George and Janet Howe

1. Ask students to open their books. Direct their attention to the text. Say: *This is a page from a magazine about television programs. It is about a new program.* Ask students to look at the top of the page and tell you what the name of the program is.

2. Silent Reading.

3. Yes/No Questions. Ask questions such as the following to elicit: *is, has, have* answers. Ask: *Is George rich? Does he have a factory in Boston? Does he have a factory in New York? Is it a computer factory? Is he married? Do they have any children? Do they have two children? Do they have two daughters? Does he have an apartment? Is it in Texas?*
Is Janet married? Is Janet married to George? Is she a singer? Is she a writer? Is she rich? Does she have a house? Is the house in the country? Does she have any cars? Does she have a station wagon?

4. Free reproduction. Ask students to cover the text. Say: *Tell me about George and Janet.* Elicit information from different students.

■ TEXTS: Charles, Patricia, and Robert

1. Direct students' attention to the three texts.

2. Silent Reading.

3. Drill: Correct my statement.

    T: *Charles is their grandson.*
    C: *No, Charles is their son.*
    Continue: *He's 38./His wife's name is Lisa./They have three children./His wife is a famous businesswoman./Charles is a bad businessman./He's a nice person./He has some friends.*
    Patricia is Charles's daughter./She's a doctor./Her husband is a scientist./She's 23.
    Robert is Patricia's sister./He's very famous./He's a scientist./His father likes his job./He has three children./He has some money./He's his father's favorite child.

4. Free reproduction. Ask students to cover the text. Say: *Tell me about Charles, Patricia, and Robert.* Elicit information from different students.

■ TEXTS: Lisa and David, Peter and Ashley

1. Direct students' attention to the three texts.

2. Silent Reading.

3. Ask comprehension questions: *Do Lisa and David have any pets? What pets do they have? How old is Lisa? How old is David? Do Peter and Ashley have any pets? How old is Ashley? How old is Peter?*

4. Pair Work. Have students ask and answer questions about Lisa, David, Peter, and Ashley.

A. Contest

1. Direct students' attention to *The Family* Contest. Explain the *true/false* activity and the questions. Give students time to complete the task individually.

2. Pair Work. Have students check their answers by asking and answering the contest questions.

3. On the board, draw a family tree with three generations and appropriate spaces for the Howe family. Write in *George*. Ask: *What's his wife's name?* Write in *Janet*.
Continue: *Who are their children? Is Charles married? Who's he married to? Who's Patricia married to? Who's Robert married to? Who are Charles and Linda's children? Who are Patricia and James's children?*
Fill in the appropriate spaces as the questions are answered.

4. Draw a diagonal line between Paticia and Lisa. Write *niece/aunt* next to it. Connect other characters to elicit: *aunt/niece; aunt/nephew; uncle/niece; uncle/nephew.* Check all the vocabulary for family relationships.

5. Check answers to some of the contest questions as a wrap-up.

6. Expansion. Give students blank cards to use for postcards. Have students write out their answers to mail in to TV News.

B. Family

1. Ask students to read the list of words.

2. Pair Work. Have students ask and answer questions using the list. Model examples first: *Who is Lisa's grandfather? George is (her grandfather). Is Patricia Howe Lisa's grandmother? No, she isn't.*

3. Ask pairs to demonstrate for the class.

Unit 12   Teacher's Book ■ 42

C. How old is…?

1. Explain the exercise.

2. Pair Work. Have students ask and answer questions about the people in *The Family*. Have students change roles.

3. Class Work. Check answers by having various students ask the questions of their classmates. Encourage students to ask classmates at random, rather than just those next to them.

D. Questionnaire

Focus attention on the questionnaire. Explain the activity.

Note: The vocabulary of family relationships is essential for students to master. However, families come in a variety of configurations in addition to the "typical" nuclear family of mother, father, and two children. Be careful with questions to students about their family setup. This is also an opportunity to talk briefly about traditional versus contemporary configurations.

E. About your family

1. Explain the exercise. Model the questions and answers in the book. Have students repeat chorally.

2. Pair Work. Have students ask and answer questions about their families. Ask students to draw a family tree for their partners based on the questions and answers.

F. About you and your partner

1. Explain the exercise. Have students write a few sentences about themselves and their partners, as in the book.

2. Group Work. Have pairs from Exercise E work with a third student and talk about their partner's family tree.

3. Ask volunteers to share what they learned with the class.

G. What's/Who's your favorite…?

1. Explain the exercise. Model the questions in the book. Have students repeat, chorally and individually.

2. Pair Work. Have students ask and answer about their favorites.

3. Expansion. Role Play: TV interview. In pairs, have students role play a TV interview. One student is the TV host, the other is a famous person (musician, politician, actor) in their country. Students can make up information as needed. Call on volunteers to demonstrate for the class.

■ WORKBOOK

The Workbook can be done for homework and checked in class. If you wish to use it in class, Exercises A, E, and Exercise I, Part Two can be done as oral pair work.

C How old is…?

Ask and answer questions about the other people in *The Family*.

A: How old is Patricia?
B: (She's) thirty-two.

D Questionnaire

Ask another student questions with:

Do you have a/an…? Do you have any…?

	Yes	No		Yes	No
brother(s)	☐	☐	pet(s)	☐	☐
sister(s)	☐	☐	house	☐	☐
cousin(s)	☐	☐	apartment	☐	☐
aunt(s)	☐	☐	car	☐	☐
uncle(s)	☐	☐			

E About your family

Ask another student about members of his or her family.

A: Does your uncle have any children?
B: Yes, he does. He has six children.
A: Does your mother have any brothers?
B: No, she doesn't have any brothers.
A: Do your cousins have a pet?
B: No, they don't.

F About you and your partner

Talk to a third student. Tell him or her about you and your partner.

A: I have two brothers. I don't have a sister/any sisters.
B: My partner has five uncles. He/She doesn't have any cousins.

G What's/Who's your favorite…?

Ask another student about his or her favorite people and things.

Do you have a favorite color? What is it?
Do you have a favorite singer? Who is it?
Do you have a favorite sport? What is it?
Do you have a favorite athlete? Who is it?
Do you have a favorite TV program? What is it?

People

The people at this party are all famous. Mrs. Vincent is a housekeeper.
Mr. Brown is a chauffeur. They're on the balcony.

Mrs. Vincent: Look! That's the British ambassador!
Mr. Brown: Where?
Mrs. Vincent: Over there. He's the short heavy man.
Mr. Brown: Oh, yes, I see him. He's wearing a black suit and a black tie.

Mr. Brown: Who's that woman?
Mrs. Vincent: The woman with blond hair?
Mr. Brown: No, the tall woman over there. She has dark hair.
Mrs. Vincent: Is she wearing a long white dress?
Mr. Brown: Yes, that's her.
Mrs. Vincent: That's Miss World! She's from Brazil.

Mrs. Vincent: There's Michael George!
Mr. Brown: Where? What does he look like?
Mrs. Vincent: He's next to Miss World. He has red hair.

Mr. Brown: Who is he?
Mrs. Vincent: Don't you know? He's a singer. My daughter has all his records.
Mr. Brown: He isn't wearing a suit! He's wearing jeans and a T-shirt. That's terrible!
Mrs. Vincent: Yes, but he's very good-looking.

Mrs. Vincent: There's Jean Collier! She has blond hair, and she's wearing a pink suit.
Mr. Brown: Yes, I know her. I'm her chauffeur.
Mrs. Vincent: Really! What's she like?
Mr. Brown: She's very nice.
Mrs. Vincent: She's a wonderful actress. She's about forty, you know.
Mr. Brown: She's fifty-seven.
Mrs. Vincent: No! Really?

44

13 People

Teaching points
Describing people
Review of: *What does he/she look like? How old is (he)?*
What color is (her) hair?
Does he/she have long hair?
Yes, he/she does. No, he/she doesn't.
Present continuous tense (*be* + verb + *ing*) restricted to the verb *wear* (*is wearing*).
He's wearing a suit./She isn't wearing a long dress.
Is he wearing black shoes?
Yes, he is./No, he isn't.
Listening for specific information.

Grammar note
This lesson focuses on describing people. The present continuous tense of the verb *wear* (*is wearing*) is introduced as a component of making descriptions. This lesson is not a formal introduction of the tense, but simply uses it as it pertains to description.
Adjective order: This is restricted here to two adjectives in the order 1) quality and 2) color.
Uncountables: Hair is usually uncountable. (Other examples are *rice, sand, spaghetti.*)

Expressions
What does ___ look like?
Don't you know?
Really!
…, you know.
Really?

Active vocabulary
about/actress/average/baseball player/beard/blond/blouse/build (n.)/curly/dark/dress (n.)/earring/elderly/figure out/glasses/good-looking/hair/heavy/height/jacket/know/light (adj.)/long/middle-aged/mustache/newscaster/orange (adj.)/pants/pink/politician/race car driver/record/short/see/skirt/slim/suit/T-shirt/tall/tennis player/terrible/tie/wear/wonderful/young

Passive vocabulary
ambassador/balcony/chauffeur/housekeeper/Mr./Mrs./party

Audiovisual aids
Cassette/CD

■ DIALOGUE: SECTION 1 (The Ambassador)

1. Direct students' attention to the picture. Give students time to study it.

2. Pair Work. Have students briefly tell each other what they see.

3. Ask students to read the introductory sentences. Then ask: *What is Mrs Vincent's job? What is Mr. Brown's job? Where are they? Who are they looking at? Are the people at the party famous?*

4. Check that the text is covered.

5. Play the first section of the dialogue on the recording (stop after "a black tie"). Then ask students to locate the British ambassador in the picture. Play the section again, pausing for students to repeat, chorally and individually.

6. Silent Reading.
   Note: Point out the spelling of Mr. and Mrs.

7. Paired Reading.

■ DIALOGUE: SECTION 2 (Miss World)

1. Play the second section of the dialogue on the recording (stop after "She's from Brazil."). Ask students to find Miss World in the picture. Play the section again, pausing for students to repeat, chorally and individually.

2. Drill:

   T: She has dark hair.
   C: Her hair is dark.
   T: He has short hair.
   C: His hair is short.
   Continue: *She has blond hair./They have long hair./They have gray hair./He has red hair.*

3. Silent Reading.

4. Paired Reading.

continued

■ DIALOGUE: SECTION 3 (Michael George)

1. Ask the following pre-listening questions: *Where is he standing? What is his job? What color is his hair? What is he wearing?*

2. Play the third section of the dialogue on the recording (stop after "very good-looking"). Check answers to the pre-listening questions. Ask students to find Michael George in the picture. Play the section again, pausing for students to repeat, chorally and individually.

3. Drill:

   T: *He doesn't have a suit.*
   C: *No, he isn't wearing a suit.*
   Continue: *He doesn't have a tie./He doesn't have black shoes./He doesn't have a white shirt.*

4. Silent Reading.
5. Paired Reading.

■ DIALOGUE: SECTION 4 (Jean Collier)

1. Ask the following pre-listening questions: *What color is her hair? What is she wearing? How does Mr. Brown know her? How old is she?*

2. Play the last section of the dialogue on the recording. Check answers to the pre-listening questions. Ask students to find Jean Collier in the picture. Play the section again, pausing for students to repeat, chorally and individually.

3. Drill:

   T: *she*
   C: *What's she like?*
   Continue: *they/he/it/Jean Collier/Michael George*

4. Silent Reading.
5. Paired Reading.

A. Who are they?

1. Explain the exercise and have students complete it individually.
2. Have students exchange books to check their answers.
3. Circulate around the room to check the answers yourself.

B. Describe people.

1. Explain the activity. Model the example in the book. Ask about the people in the picture: *What does (the ambassador) look like?* S1: *He's short and heavy.* Have students continue in pairs.
   Note: Point out that *heavy* is a more polite way to describe someone than to say the person is fat.

2. Ask: *How old is he?* Follow the procedure for 1. Call on pairs to demonstrate for the class.
   Note: Point out that *elderly* is a more polite way to describe someone than to say the person is old. *Around 35* and *about 35* have the same meaning.

3. Ask: *What color is his hair?* Follow the procedure for 1. Model the words for hair color first. After students ask and answer about people in the picture, have them ask about people in the class.
   Note: In a class where most students have the same hair color, the last step can be omitted.

4. Ask: *Does he have long hair?* Follow the procedure for 1. Model the examples and the vocabulary items first. After students talk about the people in the picture, have them ask about people in the class.

A Who are they?

These are the people at the party.

Fill in the boxes with letters A–L.

- ☐ Jean Collier, actress. Blond hair. Pink suit. 57.
- ☐ The British ambassador. Short, heavy. Black suit and tie.
- ☐ Fernando López, baseball player. Brown hair. Sweater.
- ☐ Donna, singer. Young. Orange and green hair. Skirt, blouse.
- ☐ Bradley Wilson, politician. Blue suit. Mustache. Middle-aged. Glasses.
- ☐ Doris Decker, tennis player. Long curly hair. About 25.
- ☐ Paul Cooper, race car driver. Brown hair. Beard. Green shirt. 27.
- ☐ Barbara Heartland, writer. Elderly (84). Long dress. Gray hair. Glasses.
- ☐ Robert Clifford, businessman. Very tall. Light blue shirt, green pants.
- ☐ Michael George, singer. Red hair. Jeans and T-shirt.
- ☐ Miss World. Tall. Long dark hair. White dress.
- ☐ Suzy Chang, newscaster. Average height. About 35. Short black hair.

B Describe people.

Ask and answer questions.

A: What does he/she look like?
B: He's/She's tall and slim.

Use these words:

tall   short   average height   good-looking
slim   heavy   average build

A: How old is he/she?
B: He's/She's about 20.

Use these words:

young   middle-aged   elderly   (about) (35)

A: What color is his/her hair?
B: It's black.
    He/She has black hair.

Use these words:

blond   dark brown   black   red   gray   white

A: Does he/she have long hair?
B: Yes, he/she does.
    No, he/she doesn't.

Use these words:

long hair   short hair   curly hair   a beard
a mustache   glasses

C What's he/she wearing?

A: What's he wearing?
B: He's wearing gray pants and a blue jacket.

Use these words:

| jeans | pants | a suit | a shirt |
| a sweater | a T-shirt | a jacket | glasses |

A: What's she wearing?
B: She's wearing a suit and black shoes.

Use these words:

| a dress | a suit | a skirt | a blouse | jeans |
| a shirt | a sweater | a T-shirt | a jacket | glasses |

D Who are they talking about?

Listen to three people. They're talking about people at the party on page 44. Who are they talking about?

1. _____
2. _____
3. _____

E Game: Guess Who.

1. Student A, describe a person at the party on page 44. Student B, figure out who the person is.

A: She isn't young. She's a writer. She's wearing glasses.
B: Is it Barbara Heartland?
A: Yes, it is.

2. Student A, think of people in Units 1 to 12. Play **Guess Who** about them, too.

46

C. What's he/she wearing?

1. Model the example and the vocabulary items. Have students repeat chorally.

2. Pair Work. Have students talk about the people in the picture.

3. Expansion. Ask students to talk about people in the class.

D. Who are they talking about?

1. Explain the activity. Have students look at the picture on page 44 again before listening to the tape/CD.

2. Play the recording. Have students write down who is being talked about in each conversation.

3. Play the recording again for students to check their work.

4. Have students check their answers in pairs or check them yourself.

5. Role Play. Have students work in pairs, role playing Mr. Brown and Mrs. Vincent talking about people at the party. Make sure the text is covered as they practice.

6. Ask pairs to role play for the class.

E. Game: Guess Who.

1. Explain the activity. Model the example in the book.

2. Pair Work. Have students take turns describing and guessing the identity of the people on page 44.

3. Follow the procedure for 2, except have students describe people from earlier units.

4. Expansion. Game: Twenty Questions. Ask one student to leave the room. Have the other students agree on a student they will describe. Tell the student to return, ask questions *(Does he/she have brown hair? No, he/she doesn't.)*, and continue asking until he/she figures out who is being described. Have students take turns leaving the room.

■ WORKBOOK

The Workbook can be done for homework and checked in class. For the reading (Exercise E), make sure students understand to use Part One to complete the chart in Part Two. Exercise F can be checked as a game; one student reads a description aloud and the class guesses who it is.

How much is it?

> **Teaching points**
> Asking about prices (of singular and plural countable/uncountable things)
> *How much is this pen? How much are these pens?*
> *How much is this film?*
> *It's $5.89./They're 69 cents a pound./They're $3.50 each./That's $1.29 (one twenty-nine) altogether.*
> *What size is it?/What flavors (do you have)?*
> Review: *this/that/these/those*
> Review: numbers and prices
> Review: object pronouns: *(It's/They're) for him/her/me/us/them/you.*
> Reading: Reading from a chart for specific information.
>
> **Grammar note**
> In conversation 1, *exposure* is functioning together with a number as an adjective *(12-exposure)*. Note that this is hyphenated to indicate it is functioning as one unit. Other examples in English are: a five-dollar bill, a 12-inch ruler, a four-minute mile.
>
> **Expressions**
> *There you are.*
> *I'm just looking.*
>
> **Active vocabulary**
> altogether/butterscotch/cent/cherry/cone/disk/envelope/exposure/film/flavor/glue/grape/half/hot fudge/ice cream/kilo/large/medium/millimeter/noteboook/peach/pear/point (.)/pound (measure)/quarter/regular/ruler/shake/strawberry/sundae/tape/typing paper/vanilla/what flavor/writing paper
>
> **Passive vocabulary**
> supplies
>
> **Audiovisual aids**
> Cassette/CD
> Realia: (pens, notebooks, tape, envelopes) for role play

A. Film

1. Direct students' attention to the picture on the left. In pairs, have students briefly tell each other what they see. Ask: *Where are they? (In a camera store, photo shop, drugstore,* etc.).

2. Play the recording. Check the answer. Play the recording again, pausing for students to repeat, chorally and individually.

3. Ask the following questions: *What size is the film? Is it 24- or 36-exposure? What kind is it? How much is it?*

4. Silent Reading.

5. Paired Reading.

6. Direct students' attention to the picture on the right. Point to a box of film and ask: *What size is this box of film? What kind is it? Is it 12-, 24-, or 36-exposure?*

7. Role Play. Student A is the customer. Student B is the clerk. Student B must turn the book upside down to use the chart. Ask students to role play two or three conversations modeled after conversation 1, substituting information from the picture and chart. Make sure students switch roles.

8. Ask pairs to demonstrate for the class.

9. Expansion. Comprehension practice. Have students respond orally to questions about film based on the information in the chart. Ask: *Which is more expensive, 15-exposure Fiji or 15-exposure Kudak? Which film costs $2.29? $5.59? $2.09?*

   You need 24-exposure film. Which is cheaper, Fiji or Kudak?, etc.

14 How much is it?

A Film

A: Good morning.
B: Good morning. Do you have film?
A: Yes, we do. 35-millimeter or disc?
B: 35-millimeter.
A: 12-exposure? 24? 36?
B: Uh, 36, please.
A: What kind? We have Fiji and Kudak.
B: Kudak. How much is it?
A: $5.89.

Student A, look at the boxes of film. Student B, look at the chart below. Ask and answer questions about the prices of film.

STUDENT A

STUDENT B

	disc	35-mm		
	15 exp.	12 exp.	24 exp.	36 exp.
Fiji	$1.95	$2.29	$3.99	$5.59
Kudak	$2.09	$2.39	$4.19	$5.89

47

B Fruit

Make conversations about fruit.

A: How much are the apples?
B: 69 cents a pound.
A: And do you have any grapes?
B: Yes, I do. Red or green?
A: Red, please. How much are they?
B: $1.19 a pound.
A: A pound of apples, then, and half a pound of grapes.
B: There you are. That's $1.29 altogether.
A: Thank you.

> One pound (1 lb) is .454 kilos.
> Half a pound (½ lb) is .227 kilos.
> A quarter (of a) pound (¼ lb) is .114 kilos.

C Ice cream

Make conversations about ice cream.

A: Three small cones, please.
B: What flavor?
A: What flavors do you have?
B: Strawberry, vanilla, chocolate, and coffee.
A: One strawberry, one vanilla, and one chocolate, please.
B: OK…. Here you are. Who's the strawberry for?
A: It's for her.
B: And the chocolate?
A: It's for him. The vanilla's for me. How much is that?
B: They're $1.10 each. $3.30, please.

B. Fruit

1. Direct students' attention to the picture of the fruit stand. Check that the text is covered. Ask students to list the kinds of fruit they know in English. Tell them to listen carefully to the dialogue and check off any fruit on their lists that they hear mentioned in the conversation.

2. Play the recording. Ask students which kinds of fruit on their lists were mentioned. Play the recording again, pausing for students to repeat, chorally and individually.

3. Ask: *How much are the apples? How much are the grapes? How much do they cost altogether?*

4. Drill:

    T: *They have some grapes.*
    C: *How much are the grapes?*
    Continue: *They have some bananas./They have some oranges./They have some apples./They have some cherries.*

5. Silent Reading.

6. Paired Reading.

7. Direct students' attention to the picture again. Model the names of the fruit. Have students repeat chorally. Point out that the abbreviation *lb* is used for pound weight.

8. Ask questions: *How much are the pears?*, etc., to elicit: *They're 78¢ a pound.*, etc. Say: *Ask him* (indicate student), *"cherries,"* to generate: S1: *How much are the cherries?* S2: *They're $1.59 a pound.*

9. Go over the weights. Point out *half a pound* versus *a quarter of a pound*. Ask how much a half a pound/a quarter of a pound is in kilos.

10. Role Play. Have students substitute items from the fruit stand.

11. Ask pairs to demonstrate for the class.

C. Ice cream

1. Direct students' attention to the picture of the ice cream stand. Check that the text is covered. Ask pre-listening questions: *How many ice cream cones do they buy? How much do they cost altogether?*

2. Play the recording. Check answers to the pre-listening questions. Play the recording again, pausing for students to repeat, chorally and individually.

3. Ask the following questions: *Are the ice cream cones large or small? Does he have cherry ice cream? Does he have chocolate ice cream? What flavors does he have? Is the strawberry for a boy or a girl? Is the chocolate for a boy or a girl? How much are the ice cream cones each? How much are they altogether?*

4. Silent Reading

5. Paired Reading.

6. Reading. Direct students' attention to the ice cream stand's menu board. Check through the vocabulary.

7. Ask questions: *How much is a medium cone?*, etc., to elicit: *It's $1.25*, etc. Say: *Ask him* (indicate student), *"regular chocolate shake"* to generate: S1: *How much is a regular chocolate shake?* S2: *It's $1.39.*

8. Role Play. Have students substitute items from the ice cream menu board.

9. Ask several pairs to demonstrate for the class.

D. Supplies

1. Direct students' attention to the picture at the top of the page. Check that the text is covered. Ask pre-listening questions: *How much are the pens? The notebook? The tape?*

2. Play the recording. Check answers to the pre-listening questions. Play it again, pausing for students to repeat, chorally and individually. **Note:** Point out that *I'm just looking* is an important and useful expression. When a customer enters a store in the U.S., he or she may be approached by a salesperson who might ask, "Can I help you?" or "Do you need any help?" If the customer doesn't need help finding anything and just wants to look around the store, he or she answers, "I'm just looking, thanks."

3. Ask the following questions: *How much are the pens? How much is the notebook? How much is the tape? How much is everything altogether? Does he buy the pens? Does he buy the notebook? Does he buy the tape? What does he say?*

4. Drill:

    T: *There's a pen.*
    C: *How much is the pen?*
    T: *There are some postcards.*
    C: *How much are the postcards?*
    Continue: *There's a book./There are some cassettes./There are some notebooks./There's a calculator.*

5. Silent Reading.

6. Paired Reading.

7. Direct students' attention to the exercise at the bottom of the page. Ask about the priced items: *How much is the tape? How much is the ruler? How much is the typing paper?*

8. Briefly review *this/that/these/those* by asking about classroom objects: *What's this? What's that? What are those? What are these?* Use gestures to make the distinction between near and far clear.

9. Role Play. In pairs, have students use the two boxes, Student A and Student B, to make conversations about supplies. Student A is the customer, and Student B is the clerk. Student B must turn the book upside down. Have students role play two or three conversations modeled on the conversation.

10. Ask pairs to demonstrate for the class. Encourage students to use gestures and props.

11. Expansion. Have students use realia to role play their dialogues. Set up a stationery/office supply store in front of the class. Ask different students to go to the store and buy items.

■ WORKBOOK

The Workbook can be done for homework and checked in class. If you wish to use it in class, Exercises B, D, E, and F can be done as oral pair work. Ask volunteers to write the answers to C, G, and H on the board. Check Exercise I orally together as a class.

D Supplies

A: Can I help you?
B: How much are these pens?
A: They're 10 for $1.99.
B: And how much is this notebook?
A: $3.50.
B: How much is the tape?
A: $1.29. That's $6.78…. Here you are.
B: No, thank you. I'm just looking.

Make conversations about supplies.

STUDENT A

item	price
tape	$1.29
envelopes	
writing paper	
notebook	$3.50

item	price
pens	
ruler	35 cents
typing paper	$2.09
glue	

STUDENT B

item	price
tape	
envelopes	99 cents
writing paper	$1.49
notebook	

item	price
pens	$1.99 10 for
ruler	
typing paper	
glue	$1.79

15 The keys

1.

Susan: Oh no, I'm locked out. Michael! Come here, please. No, don't turn on the TV. Turn it off and come to the door. Michael, listen to me. Open this door!
Mrs. Vega: What's wrong?
Susan: The door's locked, and my keys are inside. Michael's in there, but the TV's very loud. Michael, turn the TV off!
Mrs. Vega: What about the back door?
Susan: That's locked, too.
Mrs. Vega: And the windows? Do you have a ladder?
Susan: No. No, we don't.
Mrs. Vega: We do. Wait there.

2.

Mrs. Vega: Be careful, dear.
Susan: Please be careful, Mr. Vega.
Mr. Vega: I'm OK, but help me, please. Hold the ladder.
Mrs. Vega: Is that window open?
Mr. Vega: No, this one's locked, too. They're *all* locked.
Susan: Max, what are you doing out here? Don't do that! Be quiet. Bad dog! Now sit! Sit, Max!

3.

Susan: Michael! Do you hear me?
Michael: Uh-huh.
Susan: Finally. Open the door, please.
Michael: It's too high.
Susan: He's only three years old, you know.
Mrs. Vega: I have an idea, Susan. What about the dog's door?
Susan: The dog's door? It's too small.
Mrs. Vega: No, Susan. The keys. The dog's door isn't too small for the keys!
Susan: Right! Michael, my keys are on the kitchen table. Get them and come back.

15 The keys

Teaching points
Imperatives: *Open the window. Don't open the window! Turn on/off the TV./Turn it off.*
Be quiet./Be careful.
Help me/him/her/us.

Grammar note
Imperatives. For beginners, imperatives introduce new verbs in their simplest form (the stem) and demonstrate meaning.
Don't: *I don't know* has been introduced as a fixed expression in earlier lessons, and students will be familiar with *don't have*. Demonstrate that the intonation used with imperatives is an important factor in what message is conveyed (a polite *Please close the window* versus a harsh *Close the window!*).
Be: If overt grammar explanations have been avoided, students may be unfamiliar with *be*. Point out that *am/is/are* are parts of the verb *be*.

Expressions
be locked out
What about (the back door)?
out here
Uh-huh. (informal *yes*)
have an idea
The following verbs have appeared in the imperative form in earlier units and/or class instructions:
ask/come/complete/get/go/help/listen/look/meet/put/read/spell/stand next to/tell/write

Active vocabulary
back (adj.)/be/car key/careful/come back/chair/close (v.)/finally/find/get down from/get up/hand to/hear/high/hold/house key/inside/kitchen/ladder/light (n.)/locked/loud/move/one (pro.)/out/paper/pull/push/put/quiet/sit/through/too (adv.)/turn on/turn off/wait

Passive vocabulary
group (n.)/instructions/prisoner/story

Audiovisual aids
Cassette/CD

■ ORAL INTRODUCTION

Give a few instructions to the class; e.g., *Stand up. Sit down. Look at the light. Pick up your book. Yoshi, give your book to Yoko. George, please close the door. Maria, turn off the light.*
Note: This section focuses students on the imperative and should be done at a lively pace as a warm-up exercise.

■ CONVERSATION 1

1. Direct students' attention to the first picture. Check that the text is covered.

2. Have students speculate about what has happened. Ask: *Who is she? Who is he? Where did she go? What's the problem?*

3. Play the recording for conversation 1. Play it again, pausing for students to repeat, chorally and individually.

4. Check general comprehension. Ask: *What's the problem? What's the boy's name? What's he doing? Where are the keys? Is the back door locked?*
Note: Point out that when we substitute the pronoun *it* in the phrase *turn the TV off* the word order remains the same (*turn it off*).

5. Silent Reading.

6. Paired Reading.

7. Free reproduction. Check that the text is covered. Say: *Tell each other what the problem is.* In pairs, have students reconstruct the story so far. Circulate and check their work.

■ CONVERSATION 2

1. Direct students' attention to the second picture. Check that the text is covered.

2. Have students speculate about what happens next. Ask: *What's he doing? Where's the mother? What's the dog doing?*

3. Play the recording. Play it again, pausing for students to repeat, chorally and individually.

4. Check general comprehension. Ask: *Is Mr. Vega on the ladder? Who's holding the ladder? Is the window open? Are any windows open? What's the dog's name? Is the dog making a lot of noise?*

5. Silent Reading.

6. Paired Reading.

7. Free reproduction. Follow procedure above.

■ CONVERSATION 3

1. Direct students' attention to the third picture. Check that the text is covered.

2. Ask students to speculate: *Where are they? What are they doing?*

3. Play the recording. Play it again, pausing for students to repeat, chorally and individually.

4. Check general comprehension. Ask: *Does Michael hear his mom? Does he open the door? How old is Michael? What is Michael's mom's name? Is the dog's door too small for the keys? Where are the keys? What does Susan want Michael to do?*

5. Silent Reading.

6. Paired Reading.

7. Free reproduction. Follow procedure above.
   Note: Students may be unfamiliar with what a dog door is. Explain that dog owners sometimes make a small door in their house so that the dog can get in and out of the house by itself.

■ CONVERSATION 4

1. Direct students' attention to the fourth picture. Check that the text is covered.

2. Ask students to speculate: *What happens next?*

3. Play the recording. Play it again, pausing for students to repeat, chorally and individually.

4. Check general comprehension. Ask: *Does Michael get the keys? Does he give them to his mother?*

5. Silent Reading.

6. Paired Reading.

7. Free reproduction. Follow procedure above.

■ CONVERSATION 5

1. Direct students' attention to the fifth picture. Check that the text is covered.

2. Ask students to speculate: *Is Michael happy? Is Susan happy?*

3. Play the recording. Play it again, pausing for students to repeat, chorally and individually.

4. Check general comprehension. Ask: *What's the problem now?*

5. Silent Reading.

6. Paired Reading.

A. Role play

1. Silent Reading.

2. Model the statements. Contrast: *Be careful!* and *Please be careful.* Get students to repeat the sentences in the book as orders and as polite requests. Emphasize that tone of voice is important here.
   Note: Exaggerate your tone of voice to make the point. Point out that Susan's tone of voice changes as the story continues and she gets frustrated with Michael and the situation.

3. Role Play. In groups of four, have students role play the story.

4. Ask a group to demonstrate for the class.

B. Instructions

1. Check that the text is covered. Ask a student to come to the front of the room. Give the student the first five instructions in the book. Have him/her follow them.

2. Silent Reading.

3. Pair Work. Have students give and follow the instructions.

4. Expansion. Have student pairs make a new list of instructions, then give it to another pair to follow. Ask pairs to switch roles.

4.

Susan: Michael, are you there? Do you have my keys?
Michael: Uh-huh.
Susan: Give them to me. Put them through Max's door.
Mrs. Vega: Push the door, Michael!
Mr. Vega: Pull the door, Michael!
Susan: I have them! Thank you, Mrs. Vega. Mr. Vega.
Mrs. Vega: You're very welcome, Susan. Any time.

5.

Susan: Wait a minute! These aren't the house keys. They're the car keys. Michael. Michael! Turn off that TV! MICHAEL!

A Role play

In groups of three, role play the story of the keys. Use these ideas:

*Come here, please. Don't turn on the TV. Turn it off and come to the door. Listen to me. Open this door!
Turn the TV off.
Wait there.*

*Be careful.
Help me, please. Hold the ladder.
Don't do that! Be quiet. Sit!*

*Open the door, please.
Get them and come back.*

*Give them to me. Put them through Max's door.
Push!
Pull!
Turn off that TV.*

B Instructions

Look at the instructions. Give instructions to another student.

Listen. Get up. Get a chair. Put it on the table. Find a book. Get a pen. Put it on the book. Hold the book and the pen. Hand them to me. Go to the door. Push the door./Pull the door. Open it. Go out. Close the door. Open the door. Come in. Come here. Don't move. Be quiet.

C What?

Look at the pictures. Fill in the blanks.

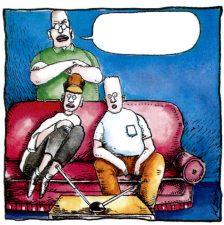

D The prisoner

This man is a prisoner in this room. The door is locked. The man has a pen and some paper. Help him get out. Give him instructions.

Answer

Get the paper. Push the paper under the door. Get the pen. Push the pen into the lock. Push the key with the pen. Pull the paper back under the door. The key is on the paper. Open the door!

Read *Story for Pleasure: Security* on page 74.

C. What?

1. Draw students' attention to the six pictures. Have students fill in each space with an appropriate imperative. Do the first one together to make sure students understand what to do.

2. Pair Work. Have students complete the spaces.

3. Ask pairs to read their suggestions to the class.

D. The prisoner

1. Explain the situation.

2. Silent Reading.

3. Pair Work. Have students write instructions in pairs. To help them get started, write on the board or say: *Get the paper*. Circulate and help them.

4. Class Work. Ask the class for suggestions.

5. Have students read the solution, which is printed upside down in the Student Book.

6. Expansion. Game: Simon Says. Explain the game. Say: *If you say "Simon says put your hands up," everyone puts their hands up. If you say "put your hands up," no one should move.* Demonstrate this. Anyone who does move is "out." Continue until only one student is left.

    A possible sequence is:
    Simon says stand up./Simon says sit down./Simon says open your books./Sit down./Simon says sit down./Close your books./Simon says close your books./Simon says put your hands on your head./Put your hands down./Simon says put your hands down./Simon says close your eyes./Open your eyes./Simon says open your eyes., etc. Extend as needed.
    Variation: Divide students into groups. Within each group, have students take turns being Simon and following the instructions.

■ WORKBOOK

The Workbook can be done for homework and checked in class. If you wish to use it in class, Exercises B, C, and D can be done as oral pair work. Exercises E and F can be checked by having students exchange books and read each other's work.

See *Story for Pleasure: Security* on page 74.

16 Directions

Teaching points
Asking for and giving directions. Imperative forms. Present continuous, in the form: *I'm looking for...*
Turn right (left)./Go straight ahead./Go past the (church)./Take the first right./Take the second left./Cross the bridge./It's on the left (right)./Go to the end of the street.

Expressions
That's fine.
Thank you very much.
Can you tell me how to get to the Grand Hotel?
You can't miss it.
I'm a stranger here myself.

Active vocabulary
across/bank/bridge/bus stop/church/cross (v.)/ drugstore/end (n.)/gas station/guide (book)/historic/ information office/left (direction, location)/lighthouse/ look for/map/museum/park (n.)/parking lot/past (prep.)/ police station/post office/public phone/restaurant/ right (direction, location)/river/road map/straight ahead/ supermarket/take/theater/town/turn (v.)

Passive vocabulary
direction/gremlin/pass (v.)/tell

Audiovisual aids
Cassette/CD
Realia: Local street maps
Note: Most authentic maps require more complex language than students have learned. Another option is to draw or have students draw simplified maps of your local area.

A. Asking for directions

1. On the board write: *go straight, go left, go right, turn left, turn right, stop.*
2. Ask students to stand up. Do a quick game of *Simon Says* (see Unit 15) as a warm-up exercise.

■ DIALOGUE 1 (A, B)

1. Direct students' attention to the map. Check that the text is covered. Help students find the starting point of the route, which is marked with an **X** and the words YOU ARE HERE. Tell students to follow the route as you play the dialogue.
2. Play the recording. Ask: *Where's Oak Street?* Play the recording again, pausing for students to repeat, chorally and individually.
   Note: Point out here the importance of using gestures when giving directions.
3. Silent Reading.
4. Paired Reading.
5. Pair Work. Have students practice the dialogue using the substitutions.
6. Ask pairs to demonstrate the dialogue with substitutions.

■ DIALOGUE 2 (C, D)

1. Play the recording. Play it again, pausing for students to repeat, chorally and individually.
2. Silent Reading.
3. Paired Reading.
4. Pair Work. Have students practice the dialogue using the substitutions. First put students into different pairs. Check vocabulary.
5. Ask pairs to demonstrate the dialogue with substitutions.

■ DIALOGUE 3 (E, F)

1. Follow the procedure for Dialogue 2 above.
   Note: Explain to students that *I'm looking for a post office* is in the form of a statement, but it is really an inquiry (*Where is a post office?*). This pattern is common in seeking directions. *You can't miss it* is a response used to be reassuring and convey that the destination is easy to locate.

continued

16 Directions

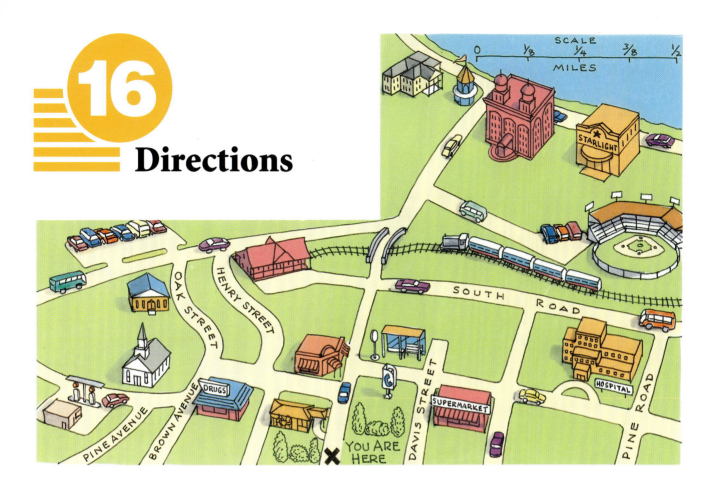

A Asking for directions

1.
A: Excuse me, where's Oak Street?
B: It's the first left, then the second right.
A: Thank you.

Talk about directions to:

Brown Avenue/Davis Street/South Road/Pine Road

2.
C: Excuse me, is there a bus stop near here?
D: Yes, there is. Go to the next street on the right. Turn right. It's on the left.

Talk about directions to:

a restaurant/a public phone/a bank

3.
E: Excuse me, I'm looking for a post office.
F: Take the first left, then the second right. It's on the left. You can't miss it.
E: Thank you very much.
F: You're welcome.

Talk about directions to:

a supermarket/a hospital/a drugstore

4.
G: Excuse me, can you tell me how to get to the Grand Hotel?
H: Yes, go straight ahead. Cross the bridge and go to the end of the street. It's across from the information office.

Talk about directions to:

the baseball stadium/the information office/the train station

5.
I: Excuse me, I'm looking for a gas station.
J: A gas station? Take your first left. Go straight ahead for about a quarter of a mile. Go past the church. It's on the left.

Talk about directions to:

the Starlight Theater/a parking lot/the museum

6.
K: Excuse me, can you tell me how to get to the museum?
L: Sorry, I don't know. I'm a stranger here myself.

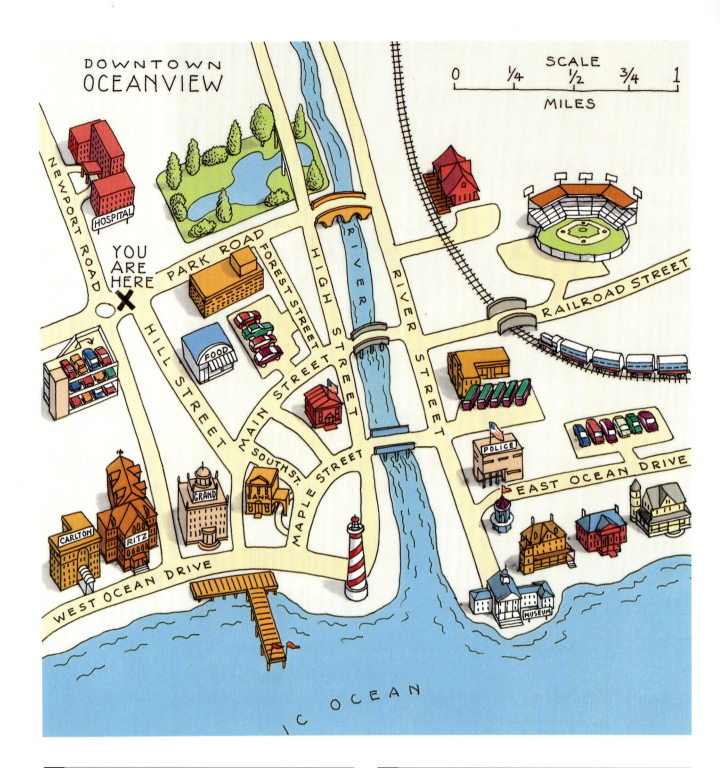

B Oceanview

1. You're on Park Road. Listen to three people. Put 1, 2, and 3 on the map.

2. Getting directions in Oceanview.
   Student A, ask for directions to:
   the police station   the Ritz Hotel
   the lighthouse   the post office

   Student B, look at the map. Give your partner directions.

C Game: Directions

Student A, look at the maps on pages 53 and 54. Give your partner directions to a place on a map. Student B, figure out what place your partner is talking about.

2. **Pair Work.** Have students practice the dialogue using the substitutions.

   Culture note: A drugstore in the United States is more than just a place to get medicine. Drugstores sell many items, such as cosmetics, stationery supplies, baby items, and candy. Prescription drugs are filled at a pharmacy. A pharmacy is usually within a drugstore, but sometimes it is also in a large supermarket.

■ DIALOGUE 4 (G, H)

1. Follow the procedure as for Dialogue 2 above. **Note:** Explain that *Can you tell me how to get to…?* is a variation of *Where is…?* It is a good phrase to use to initiate asking directions of a stranger.

2. **Pair Work.** Have students practice the dialogue using the substitutions. Make sure students use gestures as they give directions.

■ DIALOGUE 5 (I, J)

1. Follow the procedure for Dialogue 2 above.

2. **Pair Work.** Have students practice the dialogue using the substitutions.

■ DIALOGUE 6 (K, L)

1. Follow the procedure for Dialogue 2 above. Note that the response, *I'm a stranger here myself* is a common expression that conveys a sense of *I'd help you if I could.*

2. **Expansion.** In pairs, have students use local street maps or prepared simplified maps for further practice in asking for and giving directions.

B. Oceanview

1. Direct students' attention to the map of Oceanview. Give students time to study the street plan carefully. Make sure they notice the starting point on Park Road, identified with an **X** and the words YOU ARE HERE.

2. Explain that they will hear three people giving directions. For each speaker, they are to follow the route on the map and write the number at the end of the directions. For speaker one they write *1*, for speaker two they write *2*, and so on.

3. Play all three sets of directions through one time; tell students to listen carefully, but not write.

4. Play the directions again. Have students complete the task.

5. Ask students to exchange books and check their answers.

6. **Pair Work.** Have students take turns asking for and giving directions to the places listed.

7. **Expansion.** Have students practice further with additional places in Oceanview.

C. Game: Directions

1. **Pair Work.** Have students take turns giving and following directions using the maps in the book. Student A decides the starting point and destination (without telling B), and then gives directions to B. Student B follows A's directions step by step and figures out the destination. Make sure that students switch roles.

2. **Expansion. Game: Hot or Cold?** Student A chooses a destination without telling B. Student B asks for directions one step at a time: *Do I go straight? Do I go to the left?* Student A says *Hot (Very Hot)* if the move will get Student B closer (very close) to the destination, and *Cold (Very Cold)* if it takes him/her further (very far) away. Students change roles. Students can keep score of how many questions they have to ask before they can figure out the destination.

D. Maps

1. Direct students' attention to the picture of the maps. Check that the text is covered. Ask: *How many maps do you see?*

2. Play the recording. Ask: *What is the map of? How much is the map?* Check the answers.

3. Play the recording again, pausing for students to repeat, chorally and individually.

4. Drill:

   T: *I*
   C: *I'm looking for a map.*
   Continue: *he/she/they/we/Alex*

5. Silent Reading.

6. Paired Reading.

7. Pair Work. Have students practice the dialogue, substituting other titles and prices from the picture.

8. Ask pairs to demonstrate their conversations for the class.

E. Computer game: Where's the gold?

1. Give students time to read the directions. Ask: *Student A, Where do you want to go?* (the exit) *Student B, Where do you want to go?* (the gold) *Can you pass the gremlins?* (No.)

2. On the board, write: *Don't go that way./Don't go left./Go right./Go straight./Don't turn right*, etc. Have students repeat chorally and individually.

3. Pair Work. Have students give each other directions through the game. Ask students to switch roles.

4. Ask pairs to demonstrate for the class.

5. Group Work. In small groups, have students design mazes, then exchange them with another group.

6. Expansion. If maze-based computer games are available, have students work together to help each other go through the mazes. Explain that the emphasis here is on practicing giving directions, not winning the games.

■ WORKBOOK

The Workbook can be done for homework and checked in class. If you wish to use it in class, Exercises C, D, E, and F can be done as oral pair work.

D Maps

Make conversations about the maps.

A: Can I help you?
B: Yes, I'm looking for a map of the city.
A: This is a good one.
B: How much is it?
A: $2.50.
B: That's fine. Thank you.

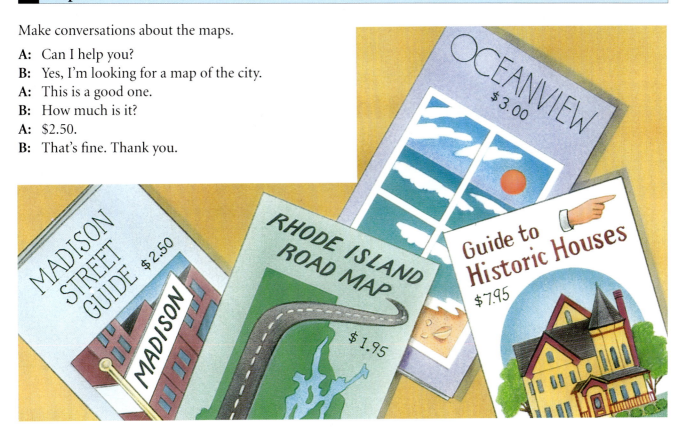

E Computer game: Where's the gold?

Student A, tell your partner how to get to the **gold**.
Student B, tell your partner how to get to the **exit**.

Note: You can't pass the gremlins to get to the gold or to the exit.

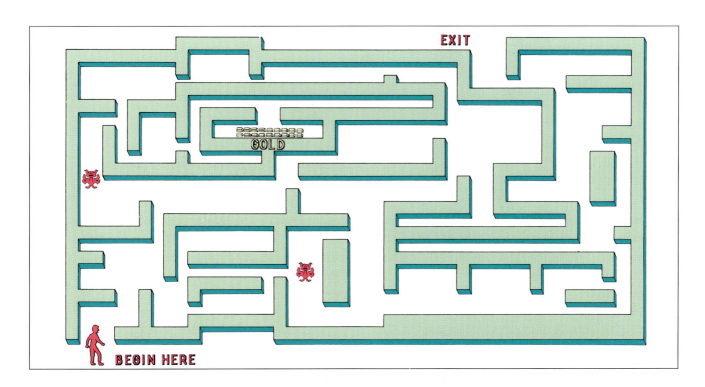

17 The Marsh House

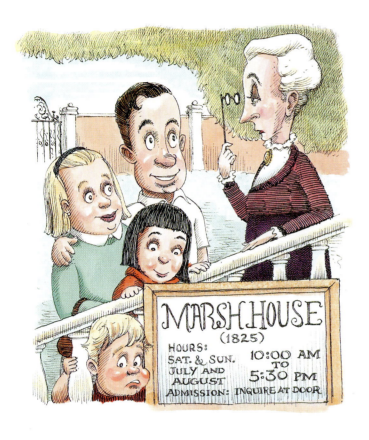

Mrs. Marsh: Yes?
Mr. Wallace: Two adults and two children, please. How much is that?
Mrs. Marsh: I'm sorry, it's 5:45 PM. We're closed.
Mr. Wallace: Sorry, kids. They're closed.
Mrs. Marsh: Oh well, come in.
Mr. Wallace: Thank you. Are you the guide?
Mrs. Marsh: The guide? No, I'm not. I'm Victoria Marsh. It's my house.
Mr. Wallace: It's nice to meet you. My name's Wallace, Joe Wallace. And this is my wife, Jean.
Mrs. Marsh: How do you do, Mr. Wallace…Mrs. Wallace? Follow me.

Mrs. Wallace: You have some very nice pictures.
Mrs. Marsh: Thank you. Yes, there are three paintings by Goya over there, and two Rembrandts on this wall.
Mr. Wallace: It's a very big house. How many bedrooms are there?
Mrs. Marsh: There are eighteen bedrooms.
Mrs. Wallace: And how many bathrooms?
Mrs. Marsh: There are two bathrooms.
Mrs. Wallace: Oh, there aren't very many. We only have three bedrooms in our house, and *we've* got two bathrooms, too.
Mrs. Marsh: Yes…well, it's a very old house.

17 The Marsh House

Teaching points
Review. Greetings and rooms.
Adjectives.
How many? How many (rooms) are there?
There are only two (rooms)./There aren't (very) many rooms.
How many (paintings) do you/does she have?
I only have one./I don't have (very) many.
Reading for specific information.

Expressions
Oh, well.
It's nice to meet you.
How do you do, (Mr. Wallace)?
Thank you. (to accept a compliment)
Take a nap.
By the way,…
Pardon?

Active vocabulary
adult/balcony/bathroom/bedroom/belt/by/closed/come in/ dining room/district/downstairs/follow/garage/garden/ how many/kid(n.)/living room/mile/only/private/ remember/stairs/wall

Passive vocabulary
admission/antique/automobile/collection/connection/ during/east/guidebook/hour/inquire/morning/public/ questionnaire/senior citizen/several/special/still (adv.)/ summer/try/volume (book)

Audiovisual aids
Cassette/CD

■ DIALOGUE: SECTION 1

1. Direct students' attention to the picture. Check that the text is covered. Ask students to speculate: *Who are they? Where are they? Who is the older woman?*

2. Direct students' attention to the sign. Ask: *How much is an adult ticket? How much are children's tickets?*
   Note: These questions are only to help focus students on the situation. Emphasize that they aren't expected to know all the details at this point.

3. Play the recording for the first section of the dialogue. (Stop the tape/CD after "They're closed.") Play it again, pausing for students to repeat, chorally and individually.

4. Ask the following questions: *Are there two adults or three adults? Are there two children or three children? What time is it? Is it open or closed?*

5. Silent Reading.

6. Paired Reading.

■ DIALOGUE: SECTION 2

1. Play the recording for the second section of the dialogue. (Stop the tape/CD after "Follow me.") Play it again, pausing for students to repeat, chorally and individually.

2. Ask the following questions: *Does the family go in? Is Mrs. Marsh the guide? Does Mrs. Marsh live there?*

3. Silent Reading.

4. Paired Reading.
   Note: This is a good opportunity to review introductions. Demonstrate the gestures the Wallaces would use in the introductions and Mrs. Marsh might use with "Follow me." Encourage students to use gestures during their paired reading practice.

■ DIALOGUE: SECTION 3

Note: Goya, Rembrandt, Vandyke, Renoir, and Manet are famous European painters.

1. Ask the following pre-listening questions: *How many bedrooms are there? How many bathrooms?*

2. Play the recording for third section of the dialogue. (Stop the tape/CD after "…a very old house.") Play it again, pausing for students to repeat, chorally and individually.

3. Ask students for answers to the pre-listening questions.

4. Drill:

   T: *There are some bedrooms.*
   C: *How many bedrooms are there?*
   Continue: *There are some bathrooms/people/ adults/children*

continued

5. Drill:

    T: *bathrooms*
    C: *There aren't very many bathrooms.*
    Continue: *bedrooms/people/pictures/adults/children*

6. Silent Reading.

7. Paired Reading.

8. Ask the questions: *How many paintings by Goya are there? How many paintings by Rembrandt? Where are the Rembrandts? Is the house big? Are there many bedrooms? How many bedrooms are there? Are there many bathrooms? How many are there? How many bedrooms do the Wallaces have? How many bathrooms do they have? Is Marsh House new?*

■ **DIALOGUE: SECTION 4**

1. Ask the following pre-listening questions: *How many chairs are there? How many dining rooms? How much are the tickets?*

2. Play the recording for the final section of the dialogue. Play it again, pausing for students to repeat, chorally and individually.

3. Ask students for answers to the pre-listening questions.

4. Silent Reading.

5. Paired Reading.

6. Ask the questions: *How many chairs are there? How many dining rooms? How many chairs are there in the private dining room? Who is taking a nap? How much are the tickets?*

7. Expansion. Role Play. Divide students into groups of three. Assign the sections of the dialogue to different groups. After students practice, ask one group for each section to come to the front of the class to do the dialogue together.

A. Guidebook

Note: The passage from the guidebook on The Marsh House is designed for reading development—specifically, to give students an opportunity to scan quickly for specific information. They do not need to read the guidebook line by line, and you do not need to explain the vocabulary fully.

1. Direct students' attention to the reading exercise below the guidebook extract. Explain that they are to answer the questions by referring quickly to the text. Do the first question to demonstrate.

2. Students complete the task individually, then check their answers in pairs.
    Note: This can be done as a timed activity to encourage students to scan quickly. Some students may be uncomfortable with not reading for every detail. Emphasize that in their own language they don't read a guidebook the same way they read a newspaper or a novel.

3. Have students ask and answer questions in pairs about Oceanview and The Marsh House.

4. Circulate around the class and listen in on various pairs.

5. Pair Work. Have students ask and answer questions about the house freely, switching roles. Encourage students to use their imaginations and invent facts about the house.

	GUIDE TO HISTORIC HOUSES, VOL. 3

OCEANVIEW

How to get there

BY CAR: From Route 495, take Exit 12. Go east three miles on Route 17.
BY BUS: There are connections by bus from New London (58 miles), Providence (39 miles), Boston (78 miles), and Fall River (23 miles).
BY TRAIN: There are trains from New London and Boston several times a day.

THE MARSH HOUSE (1825)

Location

Historic District, East Ocean Drive; the second house east of the museum, between the Reynolds House and the Austin House. (See information on those houses below.)
There is a parking area across the street.

Admission

This is a private home. Members of the Marsh family still live here. The house is open to the public during special summer hours.

OPEN: Saturdays and Sundays, 10:00 AM – 5:30 PM, during July and August only
CLOSED: September – June
TICKETS: Adults $3.50, Children $2.00, Students and Senior Citizens $2.50

Information

Designed by Charles Adams, built 1825. Beautiful gardens. Eighteen bedrooms. Home of the Marsh family for more than 150 years. Many famous paintings — look for two Rembrandts, three Goyas, a Vandyke, three Renoirs, two Manets.
Collection of antique automobiles (1896 – 1914) in the garages.

A Guidebook

1. Look at the information in the guidebook. Answer Yes or No.

1. Is the house open at 9:00 in the morning?
2. Is Oceanview 58 miles from New London?
3. Are there buses to Oceanview?
4. Is the house closed on Sundays in August?
5. Is there parking near the house?
6. Are there many famous paintings in the house?

2. Ask and answer questions about Oceanview and the Marsh House.

A: How many miles is Oceanview from Providence?
B: It's 39 miles from Providence.

A: How many paintings by Manet are there in the Marsh house?
B: There are two paintings by Manet.

3. Student A, look at the guidebook and ask Student B questions. Student B, don't look at the guidebook. Answer Student A's questions.

A: How many bedrooms are there in the house?
B: There are eighteen./I don't remember.

Mr. Wallace: That's a very large table. How many chairs are there?
Mrs. Marsh: Twenty-four. We have two dining rooms, this one and our private dining room. There are only six chairs in that one.
Mr. Wallace: Oh! What's that? It's a dead body!
Mrs. Marsh: No, it isn't. That's my husband. He's all right. He's just taking a nap.
Mrs. Wallace: Well, thank you, Mrs. Marsh. By the way, we're from Fall River. If you're there, come and see *our* house.
Mrs. Marsh: Thank you. Oh, that's $11.
Mrs. Wallace: Pardon?
Mrs. Marsh: $11. For the tickets.

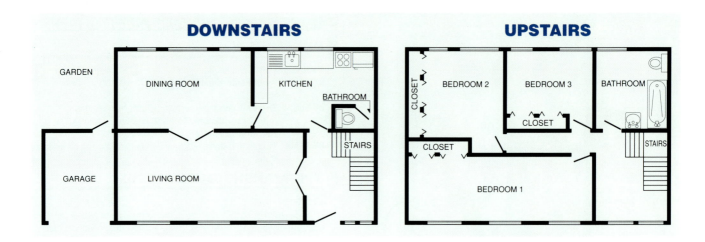

B Houses and apartments

Ask and answer questions about the house, the apartment, your house or apartment, and your bedroom.

A: How many rooms are there in the house?
B: There are eight.
A: How many are there upstairs/downstairs?
B: Four.
A: How many doors/windows are there in the apartment?

C How many do you have?

Ask two students questions. Complete the questionnaire.

A: How many brothers do you have?
B: I have two brothers./I don't have any brothers.

D How many…does he/she have?

Talk to a third student.

A: She doesn't have any brothers.
B: How many sisters does he have?

FAMILY			THINGS		
	Student 1	Student 2		Student 1	Student 2
brothers			cassettes/CDs		
sisters			English books		
uncles			belts		
aunts			sweaters		
cousins			? (Think of more questions.)		
grandparents					

B. Houses and apartments

1. Direct students' attention to the house plans. Give students time to study them silently.

2. Explain the activity. Model asking and answering the questions in the Student Book.

3. Pair Work. Have students ask and answer questions about the floor plans. Then have students ask and answer questions about their own houses or apartments, switching roles.

4. Group Work. Ask students to form groups without their former partners and tell the members of the group about their former partners' houses or apartments.

5. Expansion. Dream home. In pairs, have students talk about their dream homes, the house or apartment they would live in if they could. Student A describes the house or apartment and Student B draws the floor plan. Have students switch roles.

6. Ask volunteers to tell the class what their dream homes would be like.
   Note: The emphasis here is on developing speaking/listening fluency, not on drawing. Encourage students to listen carefully and make simple floor plans.

C. How many do you have?

1. Direct students' attention to the questionnaire. Explain the activity. Each student is to ask the questions of two other students and complete the questionnaire.

2. Write: *brothers, Student 1,* and *Student 2* on the board. Model the example and how to fill in the responses.

3. Group Work. In groups of three, have students ask and answer the questions and complete the questionnaire. Make sure students understand that for the last question they can decide for themselves what to ask about.

D. How many…does he/she have?

1. Ask students to change pairs and ask and answer questions about their previous partners. Model the example first.

2. Pair Work. Have students return to their original partners and report what they found out about other class members. Collate the results of the survey on the board.

3. Expansion. Have students find out a series of facts outside the class. First have students work in groups to write down ten questions for another group to find the answers to. Have the groups distribute their questions to other groups. Groups can then answer the questions and report their information to the class. If necessary, students may take the questions home and look up the answers.

Example questions: *How many teachers are there in this school? How many students are there in this school? How many people are there in (this city)? New York? Tokyo? Mexico City?,* etc.
How many airports/bus stations/hotels/post offices are there in this town?
How many people are there on a baseball/basketball/ American football team?
How many cents are there in a dollar?
How many cups are there in a pint/a quart?

Variation: Use the questions/answers above to have a team competition. Divide students into teams. Ask questions. A team gets a point for each correct answer.

■ WORKBOOK

The Workbook can be done for homework and checked in class. If you wish to use it in class, Exercises A, B, C, D, and E can be done as oral pair work. Exercise H *(Castle Dracula)* is designed to provide practice reading for specific information. The questions can be asked and answered orally in pairs for additional fluency practice.

18 It's mine!

Teaching points
Whose?, Which one(s)?, possessive pronouns, vocabulary review.
Whose is it?/Whose are they?/Whose (pen) is it?/Whose (glasses) are they?
Which one is (yours)?/Which ones are (hers)?
The (blue) one is mine./The (big) ones are mine.
It's/They're mine/yours/his/hers/ours/theirs/Jean's.
Reference skills: alphabetizing
Reading skills: scanning

Expressions
Do you want a ride?
That's very kind of you.

Active vocabulary
agriculture/baby food/carrot/diaper/fishing/have ('ve) got/hers/jazz/kangaroo/lamb chop/mine (pro.)/ours/physics/quasar/steak/theirs/which (one/one's)/volume (book)/yogurt

Passive vocabulary
bill (currency)/encyclopedia/floor/imagination/Ms.

Audiovisual aids
Cassette/CD
Realia: Students' own possessions. Two pens, two books, two pencils of your own. Several bags for group work.

■ INTRODUCTION: THE SUPERMARKET LINE

1. Direct students' attention to the top cartoon. Play the recording. Play it again, pausing for students to repeat, chorally and individually.

2. Ask *Whose five-dollar bill is it?* Remind students it is not *five-dollars bill.*

3. Ask students to form a line as in the cartoon. Have students re-enact the situation.

4. Take pens from two students, one male and one female. Hold up one pen, say *Whose is it? Is it his or is it hers?* to elicit: *It's hers.* Repeat with your pen and a student's, *Whose is this? Is this mine or is it his?* Take two students' pens, hold one up and say, *Whose is this? Is it (Juan)'s or is it (Yoshi)'s?* Continue at a quick pace with other classroom objects.

5. Drill:
   T: *It's my pen.*
   C: *It's mine.*
   Continue: *It's her book./It's our car./It's his notebook./It's their house./It's your tape./It's (Jiro)'s film.*

■ DIALOGUE: SORRY!

1. Direct students' attention to the picture. Check that the dialogue is covered. Play the recording. Play it again, pausing for students to repeat, chorally and individually.

   Culture note: Supermarkets in the United States are often very large and sell thousands of products. Some supermarkets feature a fresh fish market, a meat market, a bakery, and a flower shop, along with the many packaged items. Nowadays, food warehouses are becoming more common. Food warehouses sell food in large quantities at prices that are usuallly lower than at supermarkets.

2. Silent Reading.

3. Group Reading (in groups of three).

4. Take two books from one student, and two pens from another student. Ask: *Whose books are these? Are they his or are they hers?* Continue: *Whose pens are these? Are they mine or are they hers?* Elicit choral and individual responses.

18 It's mine!

Mr. Scott: Sorry! Uh, whose glasses are these?
Mrs. Worth: They're mine. Thank you.
Mr. Gold: Is this yours?
Mrs. Worth: The baby food? No, that isn't mine.
Mrs. Scott: It's ours. Thanks.

A   Game: Whose is it?/Whose are they?

Ask and answer questions about the other things on the supermarket floor. Use your imagination!

A: Whose glasses are those?/Whose are the glasses?
B: I think they're his/hers/theirs.

A: Whose magazine is that?/Whose is the magazine?
B: I think it's his/hers/theirs.

B   Which one?

Ms. Hall: Hello, Mr. Dodds. Is that bag heavy?
Mr. Dodds: Hello, Lucy. Well, yes, it is.
Ms. Hall: Do you want a ride? I've got my car.
Mr. Dodds: That's very kind of you. Thank you.
Ms. Hall: That's my car over there.
Mr. Dodds: Which one? The white one? It's very nice.
Ms. Hall: No, that's mine next to it. The black one.

A. Game: Whose is it?/Whose are they?

1. Direct students' attention to the large picture with close-ups of people from the dialogue. Explain that all of these things are on the floor of the supermarket.

2. Ask students what they see. Make a list on the board. To make the list, point to an object:

    T: *What is it?*
    S1: *It's baby food.*
    T: *What are they?*
    S2: *They're cookies.*

    Note: Students are reviewing countable plurals (*glasses, cookies, diapers*) and uncountable plurals (*yogurt, orange juice, baby food*) here. Making the list will facilitate this.

3. Pair Work. Have students ask and answer about things on the supermarket floor. Model the examples. Make it clear that the answer is a matter of opinion. Students are guessing whose things they are, and there is no one correct answer.

    Check answers yourself:

    T: *Whose sunglasses are they?*
    S1: *They're hers.*
    S2: *No, they aren't. They're his!*
    Continue with the remaining objects, asking various students to respond.

4. Put your pen on a student's desk. Say: *It's mine! Please give it to me.* Collect a number of objects from different students. Say: *Whose is it? OK, please give it to (her).* Continue.

5. Drill:

    T: *It's theirs.*
    C: *Please give it to them.*
    Continue: *It's mine./It's ours./It's Yoko's./It's his./It's hers.*

6. Role Play. In groups of four, have students role play the people in the picture, substituting different objects, and adding *Please give it to me./Please give them to us* as appropriate.

7. Ask one or two groups to demonstrate in front of the class.

B. Which one?

1. Direct students' attention to the picture of Ms. Hall and Mr. Dodds. Check that the text is covered.

2. Play the recording. Play it again, pausing for students to repeat, chorally and individually.

3. Explain *heavy* by lifting different objects in the classroom and pretending that they are heavy, while saying *It's heavy.*

4. Silent Reading.

5. Paired Reading.

6. Take objects (pens, pencils, books, notebooks, etc.) from students. Say: *Which one is yours? The (red) one or the (blue) one?* to elicit: *The red one's mine, the blue one's hers. Which one is mine? The black one or the yellow one?*
Continue, substituting *hers/his/ours*, etc.

7. Group Work. Distribute one bag to each group. Explain the activity. Have each student put three or four things into the bag secretly. Then ask the students to put the contents of the bag on the floor (or table). Have students take turns asking and answering questions, as in the examples, until all of the things have been returned. Model the examples with choral repetition first.

8. Extension. Circulate around the room and collect one or two things from each student. Return the items to the class by asking questions: *Whose is this? Is this yours? Which dictionary is yours, the red one or the blue one?*, etc. Maintain a lively pace.

C. Which ones?

1. Direct students' attention to the picture. Explain the activity. Have students look at the picture and decide which article of clothing belongs to each person.

2. Review the vocabulary by asking: *What's in the picture?* (sunglasses, shoes, socks, T-shirt, jeans, pants).

3. Pair Work. Have students ask and answer questions about the clothing/items in the picture, switching roles. Model the example first.

4. Ask pairs to demonstrate for the class.

D. Encyclopedia

Note: This exercise develops students' study skills and scanning ability. Vocabulary should not be explained. If students do not seem comfortable with alphabetic ordering, it may be worth spending a reasonable amount of time on this activity.

1. Explain the activity. Have students work individually to complete it.

2. Pair Work. Have students check their answers by asking each other about the words as in the example.

3. Check answers with the class.

4. Expansion. Ask students to work in small groups to make a list of ten words. When all lists are completed, have the groups exchange their lists and alphabetize them. The group that alphabetizes first wins. Maintain a lively pace.

■ WORKBOOK

The Workbook can be done for homework and checked in class. If you wish to use it in class, Exercises D, E, and H, can be done as oral pair work.

Work in groups of five or six. Each group has a bag. Each student puts three or four things in the bag. The other students don't look. Put all the things on the floor.

A: Whose is this pen? Is this pen yours?
B: It isn't mine. It's hers./It's Maria's.
A: Which dictionary is yours? Which one is his?
B: The blue one's mine. The big one's his.

Ask and answer questions about the things on the floor.

C Which ones?

Look at the pants.

A: Which pants are his?
B: The blue ones are his.
A: Which ones are hers?
B: The white ones are hers.

Ask and answer questions about the clothing in the picture.

D Encyclopedia

Look at this 12-volume encyclopedia.

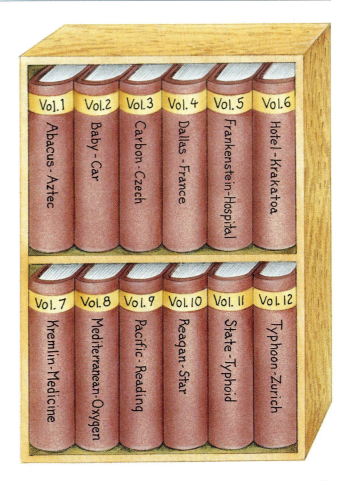

1. You're looking for information in the encyclopedia. Which volumes are these words in?

   - [ ] television
   - [ ] computers
   - [ ] driving
   - [ ] kangaroo
   - [ ] Hemingway
   - [ ] physics
   - [ ] supermarkets
   - [ ] fishing
   - [ ] the Beatles
   - [ ] Mozart
   - [ ] agriculture
   - [ ] jazz
   - [ ] Mexico
   - [ ] Seattle
   - [ ] quasars
   - [ ] the Mississippi
   - [ ] the U.S.A.
   - [ ] Picasso

2. Talk to another student.

A: Which volume is (elephant) in?
B: It's in volume (four).

Ask and answer questions about other words.

19 Asking for things

A At the music store

A: Yes?
B: I'd like *Sixteen Greatest Hits*, by Cindy Lawson, please.
A: Would you like the cassette or the compact disc?
B: I'd like the CD, please.
A: That's $14.96…. Thank you.

THE TOP TEN

#	Title / Artist	Label
1	**Sixteen Greatest Hits** — Cindy Lawson	Pacific
2	**How Many Tears?** — 4 U	Shamrock
3	**Be Quiet and Dance** — Paula Gemal	Carolina
4	**Karate King 5** (Movie Sound Track) — Various Artists	VMC
5	**It Still Hurts** — Hummer	Albany
6	**I've Got the Music** — Maria Jackson	North-South
7	**The Beginning** — Ron Henley	Pacific
8	**Hanging Out** — Corner Kids	VMC
9	**West Texas Child** — Carl Lee Hoover	BCS
10	**The Island** — Cindy Lawson	Pacific

Ask and answer questions about the Top Ten.

1. Which record is number four this week?
2. How many Pacific records are in the Top Ten?
3. How many records does Cindy Lawson have in the Top Ten?
4. Whose record is number eight this week?
5. Which group is *Hanging Out* by?
6. Who is *West Texas Child* by?

19 Asking for things

> **Teaching points**
> Polite requests and offers:
> *I'd like (a cassette).*
> *Would you like (the compact disc)?*
> *Yes, I would./No, I wouldn't.*
> *What/Which one/What size*
> *Who is (it) by?/Who is (it) for?*
> *a fifteen-cent stamp/a three-ounce letter*
> Reading: using charts.
> Reference skills: dictionary work.
>
> **Expressions**
> *regular letters*
> *Let's see.*
>
> *What's its name in English?*
>
> **Active vocabulary**
> airmail/battery/boyfriend/cap/CD (compact disc)/
> girlfriend/group (n.)/hit (n.)/ounce/postcard/stamp/sticker/
> suntan lotion/trip/weigh/what size/would ('d) like
>
> **Passive vocabulary**
> abbreviation/ask for/clerk/cost (n.)/customer/domestic/first
> class/gift/gram/mail (v.)/music store/rate (n.)/service/
> something/surface mail/top
>
> **Audiovisual aids**
> Cassette/CD
> Dictionaries

A. At the music store

1. Direct students' attention to the picture of the music store. Check that the text is covered. Ask a pre-listening question: *How much…?*

2. Play the recording for the dialogue. Check the answer to the pre-listening question. Play the recording again, pausing for students to repeat, chorally and individually.
   Note: Point out that *Yes?* is another way of saying *May I help you?*

3. Silent Reading.

4. Paired Reading.

5. Direct students' attention to the Top Ten chart. Explain the activity.

6. Have students work individually to complete the exercise.
   Note: This exercise focuses on reading for specific information. Students should be encouraged to do the exercise quickly and to scan only for the information they need to answer the questions.

7. Pair Work. Have students check their answers in pairs by asking and answering the questions. Check answers with the class.

8. Ask questions: *Whose record is number one?* to elicit: *Cindy Lawson's record is number one.*
   Who is "Hanging Out" by? to elicit: *It's by the Corner Kids.*
   Which record is number three? to elicit: *"Be Quiet and Dance" by Paula Gemal is number three.*
   Continue with four or five questions of each question type.

9. Role Play. In pairs, have students re-enact the dialogue, substituting from the Top Ten. Have students make up the prices. Alternatively, bring in a Top Ten listing from the local paper and have students use it instead.

10. Ask pairs to demonstrate for the class.

11. Expansion. In pairs or small groups, have students make up their own Top Ten list of their favorite music. It can be popular, jazz, classical, rock 'n roll, etc.

Unit 19   Teacher's Book ■ 62

B. At the post office

1. Direct students' attention to the picture of the postage stamps. Check that the text is covered.

2. Write the following pre-listening questions on the board: *How many regular letters does he have? Where is the airmail letter going? Does he get an airmail sticker?*

3. Play the recording. Check answers to the questions. Play the recording again, pausing for students to repeat, chorally and individually. Point out *Yes, I would*. Teach *No, I wouldn't*.

4. Silent Reading.

5. Paired Reading.

   Culture note: In the United States, Express and Priority mail are delivered more quickly than regular first class mail. Express mail can be delivered the following day. Priority mail usually takes one or two days. Express and Priority mail can be sent either at a post office or at specially marked mail boxes around town. They both cost more than regular first-class mail.

■ CHART

1. Direct students' attention to the postal chart. On the board write: *TV, USA, CD*. Say: *These are abbreviations*. Ask students for additional examples. Have students complete the first exercise. Check the answers on the board or have students check in pairs.

2. Have students complete the second exercise. Check answers.

3. Role Play. In pairs, have students re-enact the conversation in the post office using substitutions from the postal chart.

4. Ask pairs to demonstrate in front of the class.

B At the post office

A: I'd like some stamps, please.
B: How many?
A: I'd like two for regular letters, one for a postcard, and one for this airmail letter.
B: Where's the airmail letter going?
A: Singapore.
B: Let's see. It weighs one and a half ounces, so that's $1.74. Two twenty-nine-cent stamps for the letters, and a nineteen-cent one for the postcard. That's $2.51 altogether. Would you like an airmail sticker?
A: Yes, I would. Thanks.

16 oz (ounces)	=	1 lb (pound)
1 ounce	=	28.35 grams

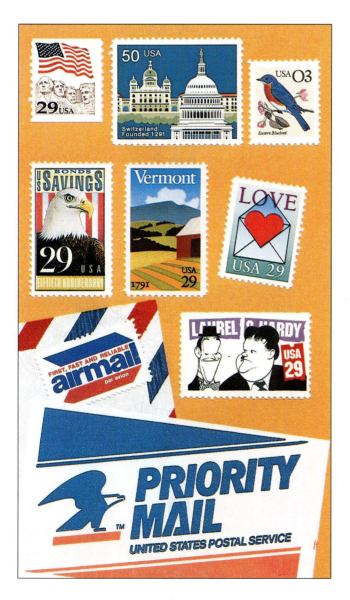

Look at the chart below.

1. Find abbreviations or symbols for:

   _____ cents   _____ dollars

   _____ ounces   _____ the United States

   _____ pound

2. Find the costs of mailing these:

   _____ a three-ounce letter inside the United States

   _____ a two-ounce letter to Germany

   _____ a postcard by surface mail to Argentina

   _____ a postcard inside the United States

   _____ a half-ounce letter to Canada

3. Make conversations with a partner.

A: How much is a one-ounce letter inside the United States?
B: Twenty-nine cents.

63

C One of those

Make conversations.

A: I'd like one of those.
B: What? These?
A: Yes, I don't know the name in English.
B: It's a sweater. What size?
A: Medium.
B: Here you go.

D What's its name in English?

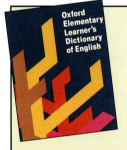

battery / ˈbat-ə-rē, ˈba-trē / n. (pl. batteries) a group of cells in a container that give electricity: *My radio isn't working. It needs new batteries.*

cap / ˈkap / n. **1.** a kind of hat **2.** the cover for the top of a tube, bottle, etc.

lotion / ˈlō-shən / n. a soft liquid for the skin: *Use suntan lotion to avoid painful sunburn.*

suntan / ˈsən-tan / n. the color of light skin after time in the hot sun. **suntanned** / ˈsun tanned / adj.

sweater / ˈswet-ər / n. a warm article of clothing for the upper body, usually knitted.

Student A, read about something in a dictionary. Describe it to Student B. Student B, guess its name in English.

E Role play

Student A, you're a customer at a clothing store. You're looking for a gift. Student B, you're a clerk at the clothing store. Look at the boxes. Make conversations.

STUDENT A		
Colors	**Sizes**	**Who for?**
red	large	boyfriend
green	medium	girlfriend
yellow	small	aunt
brown	size 12	grandfather
gray	size 36	mother
dark blue	etc.	brother
light blue		etc.
etc.		

STUDENT B
What size would you like?
Which color would you like?
Who's it for?

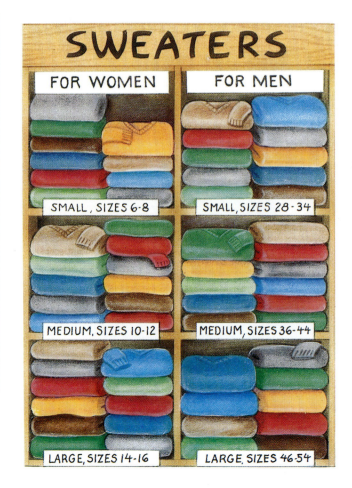

C. One of those

1. Direct students' attention to the conversation. With a student, model the conversation.

2. Pair Work. Ask students to practice the conversation, taking turns being the customer and the clerk. Have students make substitutions from the items pictured. Refer students to the dictionary extract in Exercise D below.

3. Group Work. In groups of four, have one student be a clerk, the other students customers on a shopping trip. Tell them to come into the store and ask for the items in the book. Encourage students to expand and make substitutions as they are able to.

D. What's its name in English?

1. Explain the activity. Student A reads about something in a dictionary and describes it to Student B, who guesses its name in English. First have students read the dictionary extracts and match the definitions to the pictures in Exercise C.
   Note: Students do not need to understand everything in the definitions to make the matches. Encourage students to draw on what they *do* know to make their best guesses. Point out the spelling of *its* (not *it's*).

2. Pair Work. Have students take turns asking each other the names of things in English.
   Note: Ideally, use a monolingual dictionary. A bilingual dictionary or things pictured in Units 1–18 can be used as well.

E. Role play

1. Explain the role play. Student A is the customer, Student B is the clerk at a clothing store.

2. Pair Work. In pairs, students use the boxes to role play conversations. With a student model an example to help students get started.

3. Ask pairs to demonstrate for the class.

4. Expansion. Have students make wish lists. First ask: *Would you like a cup of coffee?* to elicit: *Yes, I would./No, I wouldn't.*
   Continue: *Would you like a trip to Hawaii or to New York City?*
   Would you like a big car or a small car?
   Would you like to see a movie or go dancing?
   Would you like to eat pizza or a hamburger for lunch?
   In pairs, have students ask each other questions and write down what their partners tell them. At the end partners can give each other their "wish lists."

■ WORKBOOK

The Workbook can be done for homework and checked in class. If you wish to use it in class, Exercises A and F, can be done as oral pair work. Exercise E should be explained beforehand.

Fries with everything

Teaching points
Requests: *could* and *would*
Vocabulary for menus and restaurants. Review.
I/You/We/He/She/They'd like potato soup, please.
What/How many would you like?
Yes, I/you/he/she/they/we would. No, we/she wouldn't.
Could I/we have (the menu), please?

Expressions
A table for two
Is this (table) free?
be in a hurry
be ready to order
That's it!
Hey! (very informal for getting attention)
Hmm!
I guess…
After all
Reading: using menus.

Active vocabulary
appetizer/burger/busy/cake/cocktail/dessert/drink (v.)/ finger/fish/french fries/hot/hot dog/hungry/lunchtime/ main course/menu/omelet/problem/rare/soup/spaghetti/ turkey/vegetable/well-done

Passive vocabulary
baked/pair/waiter/waitress

Audiovisual aids
Cassette/CD
Realia: cutlery, tableware, menus, etc.

■ INTRODUCTION

1. Direct students' attention to the pictures on page 65. Check that the text is covered. Ask students to study the pictures carefully.

2. Pair Work. Have students talk about what is going on. Encourage them to use their imaginations and speculate.

3. Class Work. Call on volunteers to explain what they think is going on. Ask: *What things might they order?* Make a list on the board.

■ CONVERSATION: SECTION 1

1. Play the recording for the first section of the conversation. Play it again, pausing for students to repeat, chorally and individually.

2. Silent Reading.

3. Paired Reading.

■ CONVERSATION: SECTION 2

1. Play the recording for the second section of the conversation. Play it again, pausing for students to repeat, chorally and individually.

   Culture note: There are different ways of ordering at restaurants in the United States. At fast food places, the customer orders the food and takes it to the table. At traditional restaurants, the waiter or waitress takes the order and serves the food. Some restaurants are a mixture of these types: the customer orders food at a counter and a waiter or waitress delivers it. Or the customer orders and gets drinks and salads and the waiter or waitress brings the rest of the meal. Upon entering a restaurant for the first time, it is a good idea to look around and try to figure out the ordering style.

2. Silent Reading.

3. Ask the following questions: *Does she want soup? Which soup does she want? What does he want for the main course? What does she want?*

4. Paired Reading.